easy to make!
Curries
& Spicy Meals

Good Housekeeping

easy to make!
Curries
& Spicy Meals

COLLINS & BROWN

This edition published in the United Kingdom in 2015
by Collins & Brown
1 Gower Street
London WC1E 6HD

An imprint of Pavilion Books Company Ltd

The Good Housekeeping website is
www.goodhousekeeping.co.uk

10 9 8 7 6 5 4 3 2

ISBN 978-1-908449-12-2

A catalogue record for this book is available from the British
Library.

Reproduction by Dot Gradations Ltd
Printed and bound by Times Offset (M) Sdn. Bhd, Malaysia

This book can be ordered direct from the publisher at
www.pavilionbooks.com

Contents

0 The Basics   8

1 Accompaniments and Side Dishes   30

2 Vegetarian   48

3 Poultry   66

4 Beef, Pork and Lamb   90

5 Fish   110

Index   127

Foreword

Cooking, for me, is one of life's great pleasures. Not only is it necessary to fuel your body, but it exercises creativity, skill, social bonding and patience. The science behind the cooking also fascinates me, learning to understand how yeast works, or to grasp why certain flavours marry quite so well (in my mind) is to become a good cook.

I've often encountered people who claim not to be able to cook – they're just not interested or say they simply don't have time. My sister won't mind me saying that she was one of those who sat firmly in the camp of disinterested domestic goddess. But things change, she realised that my mother (an excellent cook) can't always be on hand to prepare steaming home-cooked meals and that she actually wanted to become a mother one day who was able to whip up good food for her own family. All it took was some good cook books (naturally, Good Housekeeping was present and accounted for) and some enthusiasm and sure enough she is now a kitchen wizard, creating such confections that even baffle me.

I've been lucky enough to have had a love for all things culinary since as long as I can remember. Baking rock-like chocolate cakes and misshapen biscuits was a right of passage that I protectively guard. I made my mistakes young, so have lost the fear of cookery mishaps. I think it's these mishaps that scare people, but when you realise that a mistake made once will seldom be repeated, then kitchen domination can start.

This Good Housekeeping Easy to Make! collection is filled with hundreds of tantalising recipes that have been triple tested (at least!) in our dedicated test kitchens. They have been developed to be easily achievable, delicious and guaranteed to work – taking the chance out of cooking.

I hope you enjoy this collection and that it inspires you to get cooking.

Meike.

Meike Beck
Cookery Director
Good Housekeeping

The Basics

Spices and Their Uses

Pastes, Sauces and Oils

Flavourings

Using Herbs

Preparing Vegetables

Preparing Poultry

Preparing Fish

Preparing Prawns and Mussels

Storecupboard Staples

Cooking Noodles and Rice

Accompaniments

Food Hygiene and Storage

Spices and their uses

Most spices are sold dried, either whole or ground. For optimum flavour, buy whole spices and grind them yourself.

Dry-frying spices

Spices are often toasted in a dry heavy-based frying pan to mellow their flavour and lose any raw taste. Spices can be dry-fried individually or as mixtures. Put the hardest ones, such as fenugreek, into the pan first and add softer ones, like coriander and cumin, after a minute or so. Stir constantly until evenly browned. Cool, then grind, or crush using a pestle and mortar and use the toasted spices as required.

Allspice, also called Jamaica pepper, is sold as small dried berries or ready ground. It tastes like a mixture of cloves, cinnamon and nutmeg. Allspice can be used whole in marinades, meat dishes, pickles, chutneys and with poached fish. Ground allspice is added to meat and vegetable dishes, cakes, milk puddings and fruit pies.

Cardamom, available as small green and large black pods containing seeds, has a strong aromatic quality and should be used sparingly. Add cardamom pods whole and remove before serving, or extract the seeds and use these whole or grind them to a powder just before use. Cardamom is a component of most curry powders.

Cayenne pepper is made from small, hot dried red chillies. It is always sold ground and is sweet, pungent and very hot. Use it sparingly. Unlike paprika, cayenne pepper cannot be used for colouring as its flavour is too pronounced.

Chilli, available as powder or flakes as well as fresh, is a fiery hot spice and should be used cautiously. Some brands, often called mild chilli powder or chilli seasoning, are a mixture of chilli and other flavourings, such as cumin, oregano, salt and garlic; these are therefore considerably less fiery than hot chilli powder. Adjust the quantity you use accordingly.

Cinnamon is the dried, rolled bark of a tropical evergreen tree. Available as sticks and in powdered form, it has a sweet, pungent flavour. Cinnamon sticks have a more pronounced flavour than the powder, but they are difficult to grind at home, so buy ready-ground cinnamon for use in sweet, spicy baking. Use cinnamon sticks to flavour meat casseroles, vegetable dishes, chutneys and pickles.

Cloves are the dried flower buds of an evergreen tree. Strong and pungent, they are one of the ingredients of five-spice powder.

Coriander seeds have a mild, sweet, orangey flavour and taste quite different from the fresh green leaves, which are used as a herb. Sold whole or ground, they are an ingredient of most curry powders.

Cumin has a strong, slightly bitter taste, improved by toasting. Sold whole as seeds, or ground, it is an ingredient of curry powders and some chilli powder mixtures.

Curry leaves These shiny leaves have a fresh-tasting flavour akin to curry powder. They are used as a herb in cooking, most often added whole, but sometimes chopped first. The fresh or dried leaves can be used sparingly to flavour soups and stews. Sold fresh in bunches, curry leaves can be frozen in a plastic bag and added to dishes as required.

Fenugreek seeds are yellow-brown and very hard, with a distinctive aroma and slightly harsh, hot flavour. An ingredient of commercial curry powders, fenugreek is also used in chutneys, pickles and sauces.

Furikake seasoning is a Japanese condiment consisting of sesame seeds and chopped dried seaweed. It can be found in major supermarkets and Asian food shops.

Mustard seeds come from three different mustard plants, which produce black, brown and white (or yellow) seeds. The darker seeds are more pungent than the light ones. Most ready-prepared mustards are a combination of the different seeds in varying proportions. The seeds are either left whole (as in wholegrain mustard) or ground, then mixed with liquid such as wine, vinegar or cider. **English mustard** is sold either as a dry yellow powder or ready-mixed.

Nutmeg, seed of the nutmeg fruit, has a distinctive, nutty flavour. It is sold whole or ground, but best bought whole since the flavour of freshly grated nutmeg is far superior.

Paprika is a sweet mild spice made from certain varieties of red pepper; it is always sold ground to a red powder. It is good for adding colour to pale egg and cheese dishes. Some varieties, particularly Hungarian, are hotter than others. Paprika doesn't keep its flavour well, so buy little and often. Produced from oak-smoked red peppers, smoked paprika has an intense flavour and wonderful smoky aroma. Sweet, bittersweet and hot-smoked varieties are available.

Saffron, the most expensive of all spices, is the dried stigma of the saffron crocus flower. It has a wonderful subtle flavour and aroma, and imparts a hint of yellow to foods it is cooked with. Powdered saffron is available, but it is the whole stigmas, called saffron strands or threads, that give the best results. A generous pinch is all that is needed to flavour and colour dishes.

Star anise, the attractive, dried, star-shaped fruit of an evergreen tree native to China, is red-brown in colour with a pungent aniseed flavour. It is strong, so use sparingly, either whole or ground. Ground star anise is used in five-spice powder.

Turmeric is a member of the ginger family, although it is rarely available fresh. The bright orange root is commonly dried, then ground and sold in powdered form. Turmeric powder has an aromatic, slightly bitter flavour and should be used sparingly in curry powder, pickles, relishes and rice dishes. Like saffron, turmeric colours the foods it is cooked with, but it has a much harsher flavour than saffron.

Spice mixes

Curry powder Bought curry powders are readily available, but for optimum flavour make your own. **To make your own curry powder:** put 1 tbsp each cumin and fenugreek seeds, ½ tsp mustard seeds, 1½ tsp each poppy seeds, black peppercorns and ground ginger, 4 tbsp coriander seeds, ½ tsp hot chilli powder and 2 tbsp ground turmeric into an electric blender or grinder. Grind to a fine powder. Store the curry powder in an airtight container and use within one month.

Five-spice powder A powerful, pungent ground mixture of star anise, Szechuan pepper, fennel seeds, cloves and cinnamon or cassia. Use sparingly.

Garam masala Sold ready-prepared, this Indian spice mix is aromatic rather than hot. **To make your own garam masala:** grind together 10 green cardamom pods, 1 tbsp black peppercorns and 2 tsp cumin seeds. Store in an airtight container and use within one month.

Tikka masala Sold ready-prepared as a powder or paste, this spice mix is used with creamed coconut and/or yogurt as the basis of a sauce for chicken, meat or fish.

Pastes, sauces and oils

Ready-made pastes and sauces, consisting of ingredients such as spices, fresh chillies, onion, ginger and oil, are widely available, but most are also easily made at home. Knowing which oil to use in your cooking will greatly improve the finished dishes – some oils are general purpose, some should be used only for cooking, while others, because their tastes are intense, work best as a flavouring.

Pastes

Balti paste Balti is a curry named after the flat-based steel pot in which it is cooked and served.
To make your own balti paste: put 1 tbsp each fennel seeds and ground allspice, 2–3 roughly chopped garlic cloves, a 1cm (½in) piece fresh root ginger, peeled and roughly chopped, 50g (2oz) garam masala, 25g (1oz) curry powder and 1 tsp salt into a food processor with 8 tbsp water and blend. Divide the paste into three equal portions, then freeze for up to three months.

Harissa is a spicy paste flavoured with chillies, coriander and caraway and is used as a condiment or ingredient in North African cooking, particularly in Morocco, Tunisia and Algeria.
To make your own harissa: grill 2 red peppers until softened and charred, cool, then skin, core and seed. Put 4 seeded and roughly chopped red chillies in a food processor with 6 peeled garlic cloves, 1 tbsp ground coriander and 1 tbsp caraway seeds. Process to a rough paste, then add the grilled peppers, 2 tsp salt and 4 tbsp olive oil, and whiz until smooth. Put the harissa into a screwtopped jar, cover with a thin layer of olive oil and store in the fridge for up to two weeks.

Korma paste is a mild Indian curry paste.
To make your own korma paste: put 3 tbsp ground cinnamon, seeds from 36 green cardamom pods, 30 cloves, 18 bay leaves, 1 tbsp fennel seeds and 1 tsp salt into a food processor and blend to a powder. Tip the powder into a bowl and add 4 tbsp water, stirring well to make a paste. Divide into three equal portions, then freeze for up to three months.

Laksa paste is a spicy Asian paste made from several ingredients including ginger, garlic, coriander root, shrimp paste, lemongrass and chillies.

Madras paste is a hot and spicy Indian curry paste.
To make your own madras paste: put 1 finely chopped small onion, a 2.5cm (1in) piece fresh root ginger, peeled and finely chopped, 2 crushed garlic cloves, juice of ½ lemon, 1 tbsp each cumin seeds and coriander seeds, 1 tsp cayenne pepper, 2 tsp each ground turmeric and garam masala and 1 tsp salt into a food processor with 2 tbsp water and blend until smooth. Divide the paste into three equal portions, then freeze for up to three months.

Massaman paste is a Thai curry paste. The ingredients include red chillies, roasted shallots, roasted garlic, galangal, lemongrass, roasted coriander seeds, roasted cumin, roasted cloves, white pepper, salt and shrimp paste. It's available in supermarkets or Asian food stores.

Tamarind is the pulp that surrounds the seeds within the large pods of the Indian tamarind tree. Dark brown, with a fresh, acidic flavour, it is generally sold dried and compressed into blocks. To use, simply break off pieces and reconstitute to make tamarind juice. It's used to add a sour flavour to chutneys, sauces and curries. Ready-made tamarind paste is available in jars from large supermarkets. Lime or lemon juice can be substituted for tamarind if necessary.
To extract tamarind juice: soak 1 tbsp dried tamarind pulp in 4 tbsp warm water for 20 minutes, then strain the liquid through a sieve, pressing hard to extract as much juice from the pulp as possible.

Tandoori paste is used on foods such as chicken and fish to add flavour and to give it a reddish-orange colour common in tandoor cooking.
To make your own tandoori paste: put 24 crushed garlic cloves, a 5cm (2in) piece fresh root ginger, peeled and chopped, 3 tbsp each coriander seeds, cumin seeds, ground fenugreek and paprika, 3 seeded and chopped red chillies, 3 tsp English mustard, 2 tbsp tomato purée and 1 tsp salt into a food processor with 8 tbsp water and blend to a paste. Divide the paste into three equal portions, then freeze for up to three months.

Thai green curry paste is a blend of spices such as green chillies, coriander and lemongrass. Thai red curry paste contains fresh and dried red chillies and ginger. Once opened, store in a sealed container in the fridge.

Which oil to use?

Groundnut (peanut) oil has a mild flavour and is well suited to stir-frying and deep-frying as it has a high smoke point and can therefore be used at high temperatures.
Sesame oil has a distinctive nutty flavour; it is best used in marinades or added as a seasoning to stir-fried dishes just before serving.
Vegetable oil may be pure cold-pressed rapeseed oil, sunflower oil, or a blend of corn, soya bean, rapeseed or other oils. It usually has a bland flavour and is suitable for stir-frying.

Wasabi paste is a Japanese condiment, green in colour and extremely hot – a little goes a long way. It is available from some supermarkets, but if you can't get it, use creamed horseradish instead.

Sauces

Soy sauce Made from fermented soya beans and, usually, wheat, this is the most common flavouring in Chinese and South-east Asian cooking. There are light and dark soy sauces; the dark kind is slightly sweeter and tends to darken the food. It will keep indefinitely.

Tabasco A fiery hot sauce based on red chillies, spirit vinegar and salt, and prepared to a secret recipe. A dash of Tabasco may be used to add a kick to soups, casseroles, sauces, rice dishes and tomato-based drinks.

Tamari Similar to soy sauce, this fermented sauce is made from soya beans and is dark in colour and rich in flavour. Usually wheat-free.

Teriyaki sauce A Japanese sauce made from soy sauce, mirin (a sweet Japanese cooking wine) and sugar.

Thai fish sauce A salty condiment with a distinctive, pungent aroma. It is used in many South-east Asian dishes. You can buy it in most large supermarkets and Asian food stores. It will keep indefinitely.

Coconut milk

Canned coconut milk is widely available, but if you can't find it, use blocks of **creamed coconut or coconut powder**, then follow the pack instructions to make the amount of liquid you need.

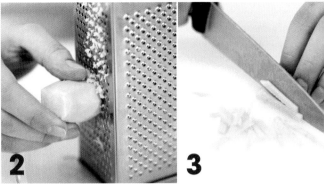

Flavourings

Many stir-fry recipes begin by cooking garlic and ginger as the basic flavourings. Spicier dishes may include chillies, lemongrass or a prepared spice paste such as Thai curry paste.

Ginger

1 **Grating** Cut off a piece of the root and peel with a vegetable peeler. Cut off any brown spots.

2 Rest the grater on a board or small plate and grate the peeled ginger. Discard any large fibres adhering to the pulp.

3 **Slicing, shredding and chopping** Cut slices off the ginger and cut off the skin carefully. Cut off any brown spots. Stack the slices and cut into shreds. To chop, stack the shreds and cut across into small pieces.

4 **Pressing** If you just need the ginger juice, peel and cut off any brown spots, then cut into small chunks and use a garlic press held over a small bowl to extract the juice.

Lemongrass

A popular South-east Asian ingredient, lemongrass gives dishes an aromatic lemony flavour. It looks rather like a long, slender spring onion, but is fibrous and woody and is usually removed before the dish is served. Alternatively, the inner leaves may be very finely chopped or pounded using a pestle and mortar and used in spice pastes. Dried and powdered lemongrass are also available.

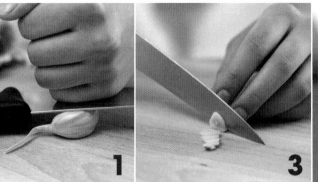

Garlic

1 Put the garlic clove on a chopping board and put the flat side of a large knife on top of it. Press down firmly on the flat of the blade to crush the clove and break the papery skin.

2 Cut off the base of the clove and slip the garlic out of its skin. It should come away easily.

3 **Slicing** Using a rocking motion with the knife tip on the board, slice the garlic as thinly as you need.

4 **Shredding and chopping** Holding the slices together, shred them across the slices. Chop the shreds if you need chopped garlic.

5 **Crushing** After step 2, the whole clove can be put into a garlic press. To crush with a knife: roughly chop the peeled cloves with a pinch of salt. Press down hard with the edge of a large knife tip (with the blade facing away from you), then drag the blade along the garlic while still pressing hard. Continue to do this, dragging the knife tip over the garlic.

Chillies

1 Cut off the cap and slit the chilli open lengthways. Using a spoon, scrape out the seeds and the pith.

2 For diced chilli, cut into thin shreds lengthways, then cut crossways.

Cook's Tip

Wash hands thoroughly after handling chillies – the volatile oils will sting if accidentally rubbed into your eyes.

Washing

1 Trim the roots and part of the stalks from the herbs. Immerse in cold water and shake briskly. Leave in the water for a few minutes.

2 Lift out of the water and put in a colander or sieve, then rinse again under the cold tap. Leave to drain for a few minutes, then dry thoroughly on kitchen paper or teatowels, or use a salad spinner.

Using herbs

Most herbs are the leaf of a flowering plant, and are usually sold with much of the stalk intact. They have to be washed, trimmed and then chopped or torn into pieces suitable for your recipe.

Chopping

1 Trim the herbs by pinching off all but the smallest, most tender stalks. If the herb is one with a woody stalk, such as rosemary or thyme, it may be easier to remove the leaves by rubbing the whole bunch between your hands; the leaves should simply pull off the stems.

2 If you are chopping the leaves, gather them into a compact ball in one hand, keeping your fist around the ball (but being careful not to crush them).

3 Chop with a large knife, using a rocking motion and letting just a little of the ball out of your fingers at a time.

4 When the herbs are roughly chopped, continue chopping until the pieces are in small shreds or flakes.

Perfect herbs

- After washing, don't pour the herbs and their water into the sieve, because dirt in the water might get caught in the leaves.
- If the herb has fleshy stalks, such as parsley or coriander, the stalks can be saved to flavour stock or soup. Tie them in a bundle with string for easy removal.

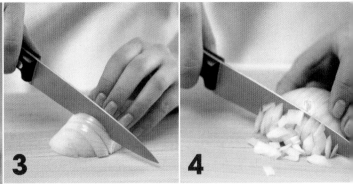

Preparing vegetables

These frequently used vegetables can be quickly prepared to add flavour to spicy dishes: onions and shallots have a pungent taste that becomes milder when they are cooked, and are often used as a basic flavouring, while tomatoes and peppers add depth and richness to dishes.

Onions

1 Cut off the tip and base of the onion. Peel away all the layers of papery skin and any discoloured layers underneath.

2 Put the onion root end down on the chopping board, then, using a sharp knife, cut the onion in half from tip to base.

3 **Slicing** Put one half on the board with the cut surface facing down and slice across the onion.

4 **Chopping** Slice the halved onions from the root end to the top at regular intervals. Next, make 2–3 horizontal slices through the onion, then slice vertically across the width.

Shallots

1 Cut off the tip and trim off the ends of the root. Peel off the skin and any discoloured layers underneath.

2 Holding the shallot with the root end down, use a small, sharp knife to make deep parallel slices almost down to the base while keeping the slices attached to it.

3 **Slicing** Turn the shallot on its side and cut off slices from the base.

4 **Dicing** Make deep parallel slices at right angles to the first slices. Turn the shallot on its side and cut off the slices from the base. You should now have fine dice, but chop any larger pieces individually.

Spring onions

Cut off the roots and trim any coarse or withered green parts. Slice diagonally, or shred by cutting into 5cm (2in) lengths and then slicing down the lengths, or chop finely, according to the recipe.

Pak choi

Also known as bok choy, pak choi is a type of cabbage that does not form a heart. It has dark green leaves and thick fleshy white stalks, which are sometimes cooked separately.

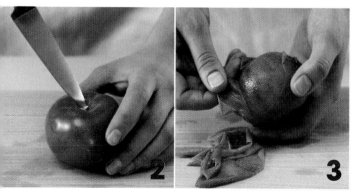

Peeling tomatoes

1 Fill a bowl or pan with boiling water. Using a slotted spoon, add the tomato and leave for 15–30 seconds, then remove to a chopping board.

2 Use a small sharp knife to cut out the core in a single cone-shaped piece. Discard the core.

3 Peel off the skin; it should come away easily depending on ripeness.

Seeding tomatoes

1 Halve the tomato through the core. Use a spoon or a small sharp knife to remove the seeds and juice. Shake off the excess liquid.

2 Chop the tomato as required for your recipe and place in a colander for a minute or two, to drain off any excess liquid.

Cutting aubergines

1 Trim the aubergine to remove the stalk and end.

2 **Slicing** Cut the aubergine lengthways into slices as thick as the pieces you will need for your recipe.

3 **Cutting and dicing** Stack the slices and cut across them to the appropriate size for fingers. Cut in the opposite direction for dice.

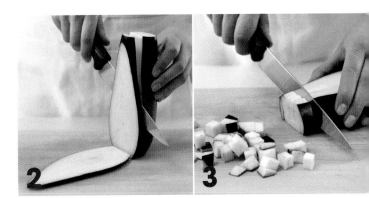

Peeling and cutting squash

1 For steaming, baking or roasting, keep the chunks fairly large – at least 2.5cm (1in) thick. Peel with a swivel-handled peeler or a cook's knife.

2 Cut the squash in half lengthways, then use a small knife to cut through some of the fibrous mass connecting the seeds with the wall of the central cavity. Scoop out the seeds and fibres with a spoon, then cut the flesh into pieces.

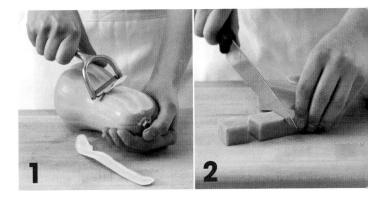

Seeding peppers

The seeds and white pith of red, green and yellow peppers taste bitter so should be removed.

1 Cut off the top of the pepper, then cut away and discard the seeds and white pith.

2 Alternatively, cut the pepper in half vertically and snap out the white pithy core and seeds. Trim away the rest of the white membrane with a knife.

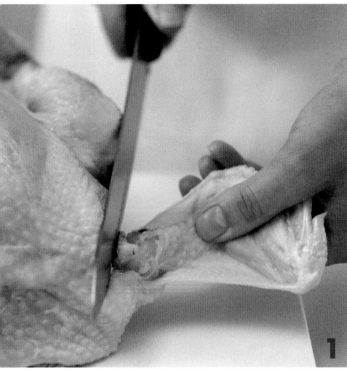

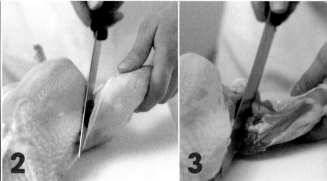

Preparing poultry

You can joint poultry at home for use in dishes, but whether you buy it in pieces or prepare it yourself, washing the bird and paying attention to kitchen hygiene are essential.

Jointing

Although you can buy chicken pieces in the supermarket or butcher, it is more economical to joint the bird yourself. Save the wing tips and bones to make a stock, if you like.

1 Using a sharp meat knife with a curved blade, cut out the wishbone. Remove the wings in one piece. Remove the wing tips.

2 With the tail pointing towards you and breast side up, pull one leg away and cut through the skin between the leg and breast. Pull the leg down until you crack the joint between the thigh bone and ribcage. Cut through that joint, then cut through the remaining leg meat. Repeat on the other side.

3 To remove the breast without any bone, make a cut along the length of the breastbone. Gently teasing the flesh away from the ribs with the knife, work the blade down between the flesh and ribs of one breast and cut it off neatly. (Always cut in, towards the bone.) Repeat on the other side.

Cleaning

Before jointing chicken or other birds, clean it thoroughly. Put the bird in the sink and pull out any loose fat with your fingers. Run cold water through the cavity and dry the bird well using kitchen paper. Wash bought chicken pieces and pat dry with kitchen paper before cooking.

Poultry hygiene

Raw poultry contains harmful bacteria that can spread easily to anything it touches.
Always wash your hands, kitchen surfaces, chopping boards, knives and equipment before and after handling raw poultry.
Don't let raw poultry touch other foods.
Always cover raw poultry and store in the bottom of the fridge, where it can't touch or drip on to other foods.

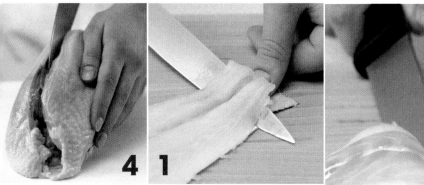

4 To remove the breast with bone in, cut down the length of the breastbone. Using poultry shears, cut through the breastbone, then cut through the ribcage following the outline of the breast meat. Repeat on the other side. Trim off any flaps of skin or fat.

Preparing fish

You can buy filleted fish from the fishmonger or supermarket ready to cook, but sometimes you need to remove the bones and skin first.

Removing bones

Although most bones are removed during filleting, larger bones, as found in cod, haddock and salmon, often remain embedded in the flesh and need to be removed.

1 Using the pads of your fingers press over the fillet of fish to feel for bones. Or, if boning salmon, drag a knife blade over the fish from the head end to the tail. You will feel the bones, known as pin bones, sticking up.

2 Use tweezers or special fish bone removers to grab the top of each bone and pull it out in at a 45-degree angle.

Skinning a fish fillet

Salmon, cod and haddock are often bought with the skin on and this can be easily removed before cooking.

1 Put the fillet on a board with the skin down and the tail towards you. Make a nick in the tail flesh, just deep enough to cut through to the skin, and lift the little flap of flesh using a sharp knife.

2 Hold the knife on the skin at a very shallow angle, almost parallel to the work surface, and work it between flesh and skin to remove the skin in a single piece.

Preparing prawns and mussels

Raw prawns can be cooked in or out of their shells. Large prawns may need deveining, or they will be gritty.

Peeling prawns

1 To shell prawns, pull off the head and put to one side (it can be used later for making stock). Using pointed scissors, cut through the soft shell on the belly side.

2 Prise the shell off, leaving the tail attached. (Put the shell to one side, with the head.)

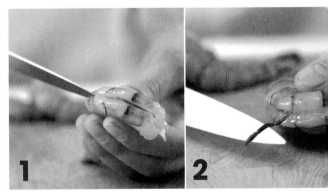

Deveining prawns

1 Using a small sharp knife, make a shallow cut along the length of the back of the prawn.

2 Using the point of the knife, carefully remove and discard the black vein (the intestinal tract) that runs along the back of the prawn.

Cleaning mussels

1 Scrape off the fibres attached to the shells (beards). If the mussels are very clean, give them a quick rinse under the cold tap. If they are very sandy, scrub them with a stiff brush.

Storecupboard staples

Noodles and rice are the perfect storecupboard staple foods for accompanying spicy dishes and are traditionally used in the cuisines of India, South-East Asia and the Caribbean. Both noodles and rice will store in a cool, dry place for up to a year.

Noodles

Wheat noodles Made from a plain wheat dough (just wheat and water), wheat noodles are a staple in China and Japan and are usually sold dried in bundles or folded into portion-sized blocks. They vary in thickness from thin strands to broad flat strips. Wheat noodles can be served in soups or stir-fried with meat, shellfish, chicken or vegetables. Common varieties include long, flat and narrow udon noodles and thin, delicate somen noodles, also from Japan.

Egg noodles Available fresh or dried, these noodles are made with an egg dough and are usually sold in nests or folded into portion-sized blocks. They come in a variety of thicknesses and are used in Chinese and South-east Asian-style soups and stir-fries. Store fresh noodles in the fridge for up to three days.

Rice noodles Also called rice stick noodles, these whitish, semi-translucent noodles are available as fine strands or flat strips, ranging in width from broad to narrow. Long flat noodles are usually sold dried and folded into portion-sized blocks, and the fine strands are sold in little bundles bound with a strip of paper. They are used in Chinese and South-east Asian-style soups or stir-fries.

Cellophane noodles Also known as glass noodles or bean-thread noodles, these very fine, whitish, semi-translucent noodles are made from mung beans. Always sold dried, they are 'cooked' by soaking rather than boiling and have a distinctive firm texture.

Rice

Long-grain rice These long, narrow grains may be white or brown. Brown rice is covered with its firm husk and contains the rice bran. It has a distinctive nutty flavour and a firm, chewy texture. White rice has been milled to remove the husk. Although tender and more delicately flavoured, it lacks the healthy fibre and many of the nutritional benefits of brown rice. Both grains can be served as an accompaniment to curries and stews.

Converted rice, such as American easy-cook rice, is long-grain white rice that has been parboiled in its husk, then dried before the husk is removed. The process retains some of the nutrients lost with regular white rice and it also hardens the grain's surface, so it is less likely to become sticky when cooked.

Basmati rice is generally considered to be the aristocrat of long-grain rices and is the favoured rice in India. It is slender and fragrant, with a good flavour and texture. White and brown basmati rices are available and can be served as an accompaniment to curries and other dishes or used in pilaus.

Thai fragrant rice Also known as jasmine rice, this tender white rice is widely cultivated in Thailand, where it is highly prized for its fragrance, flavour and tender, slightly sticky texture. it can be cooked in water or coconut milk, and is served as an accompaniment to Thai and South-east Asian dishes.

Cooking noodles and rice

Noodles and rice are the staples of spicy cooking. Often served as an accompaniment to stews and stir-fried dishes, they can also be cooked and added as one of the ingredients.

Perfect noodles

Use **50–75g** (2–3oz) uncooked noodles per person. **Dried egg noodles** are often packed in layers. As a general rule, allow one layer per person for a main dish.
If you plan to re-cook the noodles after the initial boiling or soaking – for example, in a stir-fry – it's best to undercook them slightly.
When cooking a layer, block or nest of noodles, use a fork or pair of chopsticks to untangle the strands from the moment they go into the water.

Cooking noodles

Egg noodles

These are the most versatile of Asian noodles, and are available fresh or dried in various thicknesses.

1 Bring a pan of water to the boil and put the noodles in.

2 Agitate the noodles using chopsticks or a fork to separate them. This can take a minute or even more.

3 Continue boiling for 4–5 minutes until the noodles are cooked al dente: tender but with a little bite in the centre.

4 Drain well and then rinse in cold water and toss with a little oil if you are not using them immediately.

Glass, cellophane or bean thread noodles

These very thin noodles need only 1 minute in boiling water to cook.

Rice noodles

These may be very fine (rice vermicelli) or thick and flat. Most need no cooking, only soaking in warm or hot water; check the pack instructions, or cover the noodles with freshly boiled water and soak until they are al dente: tender but with a little bite in the centre. Drain well and toss with a little oil if you are not using them immediately.

Cooking rice

Long-grain rice is served as an accompaniment and goes well with a variety of cuisines. Basmati rice is more commonly eaten with Indian dishes, whereas jasmine rice, which is also known as Thai fragrant rice, is used in South-east Asian cooking.

Long-grain rice

1 Use 50–75g (2–3oz) raw rice per person; measured by volume 50–75ml (2–2½fl oz). Measure the rice by volume and put it in a pan with a pinch of salt and twice its volume of boiling water (or stock).

2 Bring to the boil. Turn the heat down to low and set the timer for the time stated on the pack. The rice should be al dente: tender with a bite at the centre.

3 When the rice is cooked, fluff up the grains with a fork.

Basmati rice

Put the rice in a bowl and cover with cold water. Stir until this becomes cloudy, then drain and repeat until the water is clear. Soak the rice for 30 minutes, then drain before cooking for the time stated on the pack.

Perfect rice every time

If you cook rice often, you may want to invest in a special rice steamer. They are available in Asian supermarkets and some kitchen shops and give good, consistent results.

Saffron Rice

To serve 8, you will need:
500g (1lb 2oz) basmati rice, 900ml (1½ pints) stock made with 1½ chicken stock cubes, 5 tbsp sunflower or light vegetable oil, salt, ½ tsp saffron, 75g (3oz) blanched almonds and pistachio nuts, coarsely chopped, to garnish (optional).

1 Put the rice into a bowl and cover with warm water, then drain well through a sieve.

2 Put the stock, oil and a good pinch of salt into a pan, then cover and bring to the boil. Add the saffron and the rice.

3 Cover the pan and bring the stock back to the boil, then stir, reduce the heat to low, replace the lid and cook gently for 10 minutes or until little holes appear all over the surface of the cooked rice and the grains are tender. Leave to stand, covered, for 15 minutes.

4 Fluff up the rice with a fork and transfer it to a warmed serving dish. Sprinkle the nuts on top of the rice, if using, and serve.

Pilau Rice

To serve 4, you will need:
50g (2oz) butter, plus a generous knob to serve, 225g (8oz) long-grain white rice, 750ml (1¼ pints) hot chicken stock, salt and pepper.

1 Melt the butter in a pan, add the rice and fry gently for 3–4 minutes until translucent.

2 Slowly pour in the hot stock, season, stir and cover with a tight-fitting lid. Leave undisturbed over a very low heat for about 10 minutes until the water has been absorbed and the rice is just tender.

3 Remove the lid and cover the surface of the rice with a clean cloth. Replace the lid and leave to stand in a warm place for about 15 minutes to dry the rice before serving.

4 Fork through and add a knob of butter to serve.

Thai Rice

To serve 6, you will need:
500g (1lb 2oz) Thai rice, handful of mint leaves, salt.

1 Cook the rice and mint in lightly salted boiling water for 10–12 minutes or until tender. Drain well and serve.

Coconut Rice

To serve 8, you will need:
25g (1oz) butter, 450g (1lb) long-grain white rice, rinsed and drained, 1 tsp salt, 50g (2oz) creamed coconut, crumbled.

1 Melt the butter in a large pan, add the rice and stir to coat in the butter. Add 1.1 litres (2 pints) cold water and the salt. Cover the pan and bring to the boil. Reduce the heat and simmer for 10–12 minutes (or according to the pack instructions) until all the water has been absorbed.

2 Once the rice is cooked, remove the pan from the heat. Add the creamed coconut. Cover the pan with a clean teatowel and replace the lid to allow the coconut to dissolve and the teatowel to absorb any steam. Fluff up with a fork before serving.

Accompaniments

Fresh Mango Chutney

For 225g (8oz), you will need:
1 large ripe mango, 1 fresh green chilli, seeded (see page 15), juice of 1 lime, ¼ tsp cayenne pepper, ½ tsp salt.

1 Cut the mango in half lengthways, slicing either side of the large, flat stone; discard the stone. Using the point of a knife, cut parallel lines into the mango flesh, almost to the skin. Score another set of lines to cut the flesh into squares. Turn the skin inside out so that the cubes of flesh stand up, then cut these off and put in a bowl.

2 Cut the chilli into fine rings and mix with the mango cubes, lime juice, cayenne pepper and salt. Chill for 1 hour before serving. It will keep for up to two days in the fridge.

Spiced Pepper Chutney

For 1.6kg (3½lb), you will need:
3 red peppers and 3 green peppers, seeded and finely chopped, 450g (1lb) onions, chopped, 450g (1lb) tomatoes, peeled and chopped (see page 18), 450g (1lb) cooking apples, peeled, cored and chopped, 225g (8oz) demerara sugar, 1 tsp ground allspice, 450ml (¾ pint) malt vinegar, 1 tsp peppercorns, 1 tsp mustard seeds.

1 Put the peppers in a preserving pan or large, heavy-based pan with the onions, tomatoes, apples, sugar, allspice and vinegar. Tie the peppercorns and mustard seeds in a piece of muslin and add to the pan. Heat gently, stirring, until the sugar has dissolved. Bring to the boil and simmer, uncovered, over a medium heat for about 1½ hours, stirring occasionally, until soft, pulpy and well reduced. Remove the muslin bag.

2 Spoon the chutney into jars, cover and seal. It will keep for up to three months.

Chilli Chutney

For 900g (2lb), you will need:
900g (2lb) very ripe tomatoes, roughly chopped, 8 red chillies, seeded (see page 15), 6 garlic cloves, crushed, 5cm (2in) piece fresh root ginger, grated, 1 lemongrass stalk, trimmed and outer layer removed, 1 star anise, 550g (1¼lb) golden caster sugar, 200ml (7fl oz) red wine vinegar.

1 Put half the tomatoes into a food processor or blender. Roughly chop the chillies, add to the blender with the garlic and ginger and blend to a purée. Transfer to a heavy-based pan.

2 Crush the lemongrass and cut in half. Tie the cut halves together with string, then add to the pan with the star anise, sugar and vinegar.

3 Bring the mixture to the boil, add the remaining tomatoes, then reduce the heat. Cook gently for 45–50 minutes, stirring occasionally and skimming off any foam, until the mixture has thickened and reduced slightly. Remove the star anise and lemongrass.

4 Spoon the chutney into jars, cover and seal. Chill and use within one month.

Fresh Coriander Chutney

For 275g (10oz), you will need:
100g (3½oz) fresh coriander, washed and dried, 1 medium onion, roughly chopped, 2 fresh green chillies, seeded (see page 15), 2.5cm (1in) piece fresh root ginger, peeled, 1 tsp salt, 2 tbsp lemon or lime juice, 1 tbsp desiccated coconut.

1 Put all the ingredients in a blender or food processor and blend until smooth.

2 Transfer to a glass or plastic bowl, cover and chill in the fridge. It will keep for up to one week.

Food hygiene and storage

Storing food properly and preparing it in a hygienic way is important to ensure that food remains as nutritious and flavourful as possible, and to reduce the risk of food poisoning.

Hygiene

When you are preparing food, always follow these important guidelines for cleanliness in the kitchen:

Wash your hands thoroughly before handling food and again between handling different types of food, such as raw and cooked meat and poultry. If you have any cuts or grazes on your hands, be sure to keep them covered with a waterproof plaster.

Wash down worksurfaces regularly with a mild detergent solution or multi-surface cleaner.

Use a dishwasher if available. Otherwise, wear rubber gloves for washing-up, so that the water temperature can be hotter than unprotected hands can bear. Change drying-up cloths and cleaning cloths regularly. Note that leaving dishes to drain is more hygienic than drying them with a teatowel.

Keep raw and cooked foods separate, especially meat, fish and poultry. Wash kitchen utensils in between preparing raw and cooked foods. Never put cooked or ready-to-eat foods directly on to a surface that has just had raw fish, meat or poultry on it. See also Poultry Hygiene on page 20.

Keep pets out of the kitchen if possible; or make sure they stay away from worksurfaces. Never allow animals on to worksurfaces.

Shopping

Always choose fresh ingredients in prime condition from stores and markets that have a regular turnover of stock to ensure you buy the freshest produce possible.

Make sure items are within their 'best before' or 'use by' date. (Foods with a longer shelf life have a 'best before' date; more perishable items have a 'use by' date.)

Pack frozen and chilled items in an insulated cool bag at the check-out and put them into the freezer or fridge as soon as you get home.

During warm weather in particular, buy perishable foods just before you return home. When packing items at the check-out, sort them according to where you will store them when you get home – the storecupboard, fridge, freezer, vegetable rack, fruit bowl, and so on. This will make unpacking easier – and quicker.

The storecupboard

Although storecupboard ingredients will generally last a long time, correct storage is important:

Always check packaging for storage advice – even with familiar foods, because storage requirements may change if additives, sugar or salt have been reduced. Check storecupboard foods for their 'best before' or 'use by' date and do not use them if the date has passed.

Keep all food cupboards scrupulously clean and make sure food containers and packs are properly sealed.

Once opened, treat canned foods as though fresh. Always transfer the contents to a clean container, cover and keep in the fridge. Similarly, jars, sauce bottles and cartons should be kept chilled after opening. (Check the label for safe storage times after opening.)

Transfer dry goods such as sugar, flour, rice and pasta to moisture-proof containers. When supplies are used up, wash the container well and thoroughly dry before refilling with new supplies.

Store oils in a dark cupboard away from any heat source, as heat and light can make them turn rancid and affect their colour. For the same reason, buy olive oil in dark green bottles.

Store vinegars in a cool place; they can turn bad in a warm environment.

Store dried herbs, spices and flavourings in a cool, dark cupboard or in dark jars. Buy in small quantities as their flavour will not last indefinitely.

Fridge storage

Fresh food needs to be kept in the cool temperature of the fridge to keep it in good condition and discourage the growth of harmful bacteria. Store day-to-day perishable items, such as opened jams and jellies, mayonnaise and bottled sauces, in the fridge along with eggs and dairy products, fruit juices, bacon, fresh and cooked meat (on separate shelves), and salads and vegetables (except potatoes, which don't suit being stored in the cold). A fridge should be kept at an operating temperature of 4–5°C. It is worth investing in a fridge thermometer to ensure the correct temperature is maintained.

To ensure your fridge is functioning effectively for safe food storage, follow these guidelines:

To avoid bacterial cross-contamination, store cooked and raw foods on separate shelves, putting cooked foods on the top shelf. Ensure that all items are well wrapped.

Never put hot food into the fridge, as this will cause the internal temperature of the fridge to rise.

Avoid overfilling the fridge, as this restricts the circulation of air and prevents the appliance from working properly.

It can take some time for the fridge to return to the correct operating temperature once the door has been opened, so don't leave it open any longer than is necessary.

Clean the fridge regularly, using a specially formulated germicidal fridge cleaner. Alternatively, use a weak solution of bicarbonate of soda: 1 tbsp to 1 litre (1³/₄ pints) water.

If your fridge doesn't have an automatic defrost facility, defrost regularly.

Maximum fridge storage times

For pre-packed foods, always adhere to the 'use by' date on the pack. For other foods the following storage times should apply, providing the food is in prime condition when it goes into the fridge and that your fridge is in good working order:

Vegetables

Green vegetables	3–4 days
Salad leaves	2–3 days

Dairy Food

Eggs	1 week
Milk	4–5 days

Fish

Fish	1 day
Shellfish	1 day

Raw Meat

Bacon	7 days
Game	2 days
Minced meat	1 day
Offal	1 day
Poultry	2 days
Raw sliced meat	2 days

Cooked Meat

Sliced meat	2 days
Ham	2 days
Ham, vacuum-packed (or according to the instructions on the pack)	1–2 weeks

1

Accompaniments and side dishes

Warm Spiced Rice Salad

Melon, Mango and Cucumber Salad

Thai Crab Balls with Sweet Chilli Sauce

Prawn Poppadoms

Lime and Chilli Chicken Goujons

Sag Aloo

Aubergine and Chickpea Pilaf

Oven-baked Chilli Rice

Vegetable Samosas

Onion Bhajis

Pakoras

Cumin Courgettes with Paneer

Dal with Aubergine and Mushrooms

Try Something Different
- -

Replace the goat's cheese with two roasted, skinless chicken breasts, which have been shredded.

Warm Spiced Rice Salad

½ tbsp ground cumin

½ tsp ground cinnamon

2 tbsp sunflower oil

2 large red onions, sliced

250g (9oz) basmati rice

600ml (1 pint) hot vegetable or chicken stock

400g can lentils, drained and rinsed

salt and ground black pepper

For the salad

75g (3oz) watercress

250g (9oz) broccoli, steamed and chopped into 2.5cm (1in) pieces

25g (1oz) sultanas

75g (3oz) ready-to-eat dried apricots, chopped

75g (3oz) mixed nuts and seeds

2 tbsp freshly chopped flat-leafed parsley

100g (3½oz) goat's cheese, crumbled

1 Put the cumin and cinnamon into a large, deep frying pan and heat gently for 1–2 minutes. Add the oil and onions and fry over a low heat for 8–10 minutes until the onions are soft. Add the rice, toss to coat in the spices and onions, then add the hot stock. Cover and cook for 12–15 minutes until the stock has been absorbed and the rice is cooked. Season, tip into a serving bowl and add the lentils.

2 To make the salad, add the watercress, broccoli, sultanas, apricots and mixed nuts and seeds to the bowl. Scatter with the parsley, then toss together, top with the cheese and serve immediately.

Serves 4	EASY		NUTRITIONAL INFORMATION	
	Preparation Time 10 minutes	**Cooking Time** 20–30 minutes	**Per Serving** 700 calories, 27g fat (of which 6g saturates), 88g carbohydrate, 0.7g salt	Vegetarian Gluten free

Get Ahead

Complete the recipe, store in an airtight container and chill. It will keep for up to one day.

½ cucumber, halved lengthways and seeded

1 Charentais melon, halved and seeded

1 mango, peeled and stoned

freshly chopped flat-leafed parsley and lime wedges to serve

For the wasabi dressing

3 tsp tamari or light soy sauce

1 tbsp dry sherry

1 tbsp rice wine vinegar or white wine vinegar

¼ tsp wasabi paste or finely chopped green chilli

Melon, Mango and Cucumber Salad

1 Cut the cucumber into slim diagonal slices. Cut the rind off the melon and cut the flesh into pieces that are a similar size to the cucumber slices. Cut the mango flesh into similar-sized lengths. Mix the cucumber, melon and mango in a large bowl.

2 Whisk all the ingredients for the wasabi dressing in a small bowl, then pour over the salad and toss gently. Sprinkle with chopped flat-leafed parsley and serve with lime wedges.

EASY	NUTRITIONAL INFORMATION		Serves
Preparation Time 15 minutes, plus chilling	**Per Serving** 62 calories, trace fat, 14g carbohydrate, 1.5g salt	Vegetarian Dairy free	**6**

Thai Crab Balls with Sweet Chilli Sauce

2 tsp sesame oil

1 large red chilli, seeded and finely chopped (see page 15)

2.5cm (1in) piece fresh root ginger, peeled and finely grated, plus 2 tbsp finely chopped fresh root ginger

2 garlic cloves, crushed

8 tbsp light muscovado sugar

3 tsp Thai fish sauce (nam pla)

2 tbsp light soy sauce

juice of 2 limes

1 tbsp sunflower oil, plus extra for deep-frying

4 spring onions, finely chopped

1 lemongrass stalk, outer leaves discarded and remainder finely chopped

350g (12oz) fresh or frozen crabmeat

2 tbsp freshly chopped coriander

75g (3oz) white breadcrumbs

3 medium eggs

ground black pepper

50g (2oz) plain flour

fresh coriander sprigs, shredded red chilli and lime wedges to garnish

1 To make the sweet chilli sauce, put the sesame oil in a pan and heat gently. Add ½ tsp chopped chilli, 2 tbsp chopped ginger and 1 garlic clove, and cook for 1–2 minutes until softened. Add the sugar, 2 tsp fish sauce and the soy sauce, then bring to the boil, reduce the heat and simmer for 2 minutes. Remove from the heat and stir in 8 tbsp water and the lime juice. Pour into a serving bowl, cover and put to one side.

2 To make the crab balls, heat 1 tbsp sunflower oil in a small pan and add the spring onions, the grated ginger, remaining chilli and garlic and the lemongrass. Cook gently for 2–3 minutes until soft. Transfer to a bowl and cool, then stir in the crabmeat, coriander, remaining fish sauce, 6 tbsp breadcrumbs and 1 egg. Mix and season with pepper only. Shape tablespoonfuls of the mixture into 18 balls, put on a baking sheet and chill for 20 minutes.

3 Beat the remaining eggs. Coat each ball lightly with flour, roll them in the beaten eggs, then in the remaining breadcrumbs. Heat the sunflower oil in a large pan and deep-fry the crab balls in batches for 3–4 minutes or until golden. Drain on kitchen paper and keep warm while frying the remaining balls. Garnish with coriander sprigs, shredded red chilli and lime wedges, and serve with the sweet chilli sauce.

A LITTLE EFFORT		NUTRITIONAL INFORMATION		Makes
Preparation Time 30 minutes, plus chilling	**Cooking Time** 20 minutes	**Per Ball with Sauce** 127 calories, 6.8g fat (of which 1g saturates), 11.1g carbohydrate, 0.8g salt	Dairy free	**18** Balls

Prawn Poppadoms

24 raw tiger prawns, peeled and deveined (see page 22)

4 tbsp Sweet Chilli Sauce (see step 2, page 112)

$^{1}/_{2}$ tbsp sesame oil

150ml ($^{1}/_{4}$ pint) soured cream

24 mini poppadoms

1 lime, cut into thin wedges, to serve

1 Quickly fry the prawns with 2 tbsp sweet chilli sauce and the sesame oil for 3–4 minutes until just pink.

2 Mix the remaining sweet chilli sauce with the soured cream, then spoon on to the poppadoms. Top each with a prawn and a sliver of fresh lime (assemble just before serving, otherwise the poppadoms will go soft).

Makes	EASY		NUTRITIONAL INFORMATION	
24	**Preparation Time** 10 minutes	**Cooking Time** 3 minutes	**Per Serving** 57 calories, 3.1g fat (of which 1.1g saturates), 4.2g carbohydrate, 0.2g salt	Gluten free

Cook's Tip

For a lower-fat version of this recipe, bake the goujons in the oven. Preheat the oven to 200°C (180°C fan oven) mark 6. Put the goujons on a lightly oiled baking sheet, brush each with a little oil and bake for 12–15 minutes until golden and cooked through.

Lime and Chilli Chicken Goujons

300g (11oz) skinless, boneless chicken thighs
50g (2oz) fresh breadcrumbs
50g (2oz) plain flour
2 tsp dried chilli flakes
grated zest of 1 lime
1 tsp salt
1 medium egg, beaten
2 tbsp sunflower oil
lime wedges to serve

For the dip
6 tbsp natural yogurt
6 tbsp mayonnaise
¼ cucumber, halved, seeded and finely diced
25g (1oz) freshly chopped coriander
juice of 1 lime
salt and ground black pepper

1 Put all the ingredients for the dip into a bowl. Season with salt and pepper and mix well, then chill.

2 Cut the chicken into strips. Put the breadcrumbs into a bowl with the flour, chilli flakes, lime zest and salt. Mix well. Pour the egg on to a plate. Dip the chicken strips into the egg, then coat in the breadcrumb mixture.

3 Heat the oil in a frying pan over a medium heat. Fry the chicken in batches for 7–10 minutes until golden and cooked through. Keep warm while cooking the remainder. Transfer to a serving plate, sprinkle with a little salt, then serve with the dip and lime wedges.

EASY		NUTRITIONAL INFORMATION	Serves
Preparation Time 15 minutes	**Cooking Time** 20 minutes	**Per Serving** 420 calories, 28.7g fat (of which 5g saturates), 21.9g carbohydrate, 2g salt	**4**

Saag Aloo

2–3 tbsp vegetable oil

1 onion, finely sliced

2 garlic cloves, finely chopped

1 tbsp black mustard seeds

2 tsp ground turmeric

900g (2lb) potatoes, peeled and cut
into 4cm (½in) chunks

1 tsp salt

4 handfuls baby spinach leaves

1 Heat the oil in a pan and fry the onion over a medium heat for 10 minutes until golden, taking care not to burn it.

2 Add the garlic, mustard seeds and turmeric and cook for 1 minute. Add the potatoes, salt and 150ml (¼ pint) water. Cover the pan, bring to the boil, then reduce the heat and cook gently for 35–40 minutes or until tender. Add the spinach and cook until the leaves just wilt. Serve immediately.

Serves	EASY		NUTRITIONAL INFORMATION	
4	**Preparation Time** 15 minutes	**Cooking Time** 55 minutes	**Per Serving** 295 calories, 10.2g fat (of which 1.2g saturates), 46.7g carbohydrate, 0.2g salt	Vegetarian Gluten free • Dairy free

Get Ahead

To prepare ahead, fry the aubergine and onion as in step 1. Cover and keep in a cool place for 1½ hours.
To use Complete the recipe.

4–6 tbsp olive oil

275g (10oz) aubergine, roughly chopped

225g (8oz) onions, finely chopped

25g (1oz) butter

½ tsp cumin seeds

175g (6oz) long-grain rice

600ml (1 pint) vegetable or chicken stock

400g can chickpeas, drained and rinsed

225g (8oz) baby spinach leaves

salt and ground black pepper

Aubergine and Chickpea Pilaf

1 Heat half the oil in a large pan or flameproof casserole over a medium heat. Fry the aubergine for 4–5 minutes, in batches, until deep golden brown. Remove from the pan with a slotted spoon and put to one side. Add the remaining oil to the pan, then add the onions and cook for 5 minutes or until golden and soft.

2 Add the butter, then stir in the cumin seeds and rice. Fry for 1–2 minutes. Pour in the stock, season with salt and pepper and bring to the boil. Reduce the heat, then simmer, uncovered, for 10–12 minutes until most of the liquid has evaporated and the rice is tender.

3 Remove the pan from the heat. Stir in the chickpeas, spinach and reserved aubergine. Cover with a tight-fitting lid and leave to stand for 5 minutes until the spinach has wilted and the chickpeas are heated through. Adjust the seasoning to taste. Fork through the rice grains to separate and make the rice fluffy before serving.

EASY		NUTRITIONAL INFORMATION		Serves
Preparation Time 10 minutes	**Cooking Time** 20 minutes, plus 5 minutes standing	**Per Serving** 462 calories, 20g fat (of which 5g saturates), 58g carbohydrate, 0.9g salt	Vegetarian Gluten free	**4**

Oven-baked Chilli Rice

3 tbsp olive oil

1 large red onion, thinly sliced

1 red chilli, seeded and thinly sliced (see page 15)

1 tbsp tamarind paste

1 tbsp light muscovado sugar

350g (12oz) mixed basmati and wild rice

a little oil or butter to grease

20g pack fresh mint, roughly chopped

100g bag baby leaf spinach

50g (2oz) flaked almonds, toasted
(see Cook's Tips, page 108)

salt and ground black pepper

1 Heat the oil in a frying pan and fry the onion for 7–10 minutes over a medium heat until golden and soft. Add the chilli, tamarind paste and sugar. Cool, cover and chill.

2 Meanwhile, put the rice in a large pan. Add 800ml (1 pint 7fl oz) boiling water. Cover and bring to the boil, then turn the heat to its lowest setting and cook according to the pack instructions. Spread on a baking sheet and leave to cool, then chill.

3 When ready to serve, preheat the oven to 200°C (180°C fan oven) mark 6. Tip the rice into a lightly greased, shallow ovenproof dish. Stir in the onion mixture and season with salt and pepper.

4 Reheat the rice in the oven for 20 minutes until piping hot. Stir in the mint, spinach and almonds and serve immediately.

Serves	EASY		NUTRITIONAL INFORMATION	
8	**Preparation Time** 15 minutes, plus chilling	**Cooking Time** 40 minutes	**Per Serving** 265 calories, 8.1g fat (of which 0.9g saturates), 42.2g carbohydrate, 0.1g salt	Vegetarian Gluten free • Dairy free

Cook's Tip

Samosa Pastry Mix together 450g (1lb) plain flour, 1 tsp salt and 3 tbsp freshly chopped coriander. Add 4 tbsp vegetable oil, melted ghee or butter and about 200ml (7fl oz) warm water to make a soft dough. Knead on a lightly floured surface for 5 minutes. While using, keep covered with a damp cloth to prevent drying out.

Vegetable Samosas

450g (1lb) potatoes, peeled and halved

1 tbsp vegetable oil, plus extra for deep-frying

1 onion, finely chopped

1 garlic clove, crushed

1–2 hot green chillies, seeded, if you like, and chopped (see page 15)

2 tsp each ground coriander and cumin seeds

1 tsp ground fenugreek

1 large ripe tomato, chopped

50g (2oz) frozen peas

2 tbsp freshly chopped coriander

1 tbsp freshly chopped mint

Samosa Pastry (see Cook's Tip)

salt and ground black pepper

mint sprigs and lime halves to garnish

1 Cook the potatoes in salted water until just tender. Drain and chop into fairly small pieces. Heat the oil in a frying pan. Add the onion and garlic and cook for about 5 minutes until softened. Add the spices and cook for 2 minutes, stirring all the time. Add the tomato to the pan and simmer until softened. Add the potatoes and stir to coat in the spice mixture. Add the peas and cook for 1–2 minutes until thawed. Add the herbs and seasoning. Leave to cool.

2 Divide the Samosa Pastry into 12 pieces. Roll one piece out to a 15cm (6in) round. Cut in half, then put a heaped teaspoon of filling on to each half. Dampen the edges, fold over the filling and press together to seal. Repeat with remaining pastry.

3 Heat the oil for deep-frying to 180°C (test by frying a small cube of bread; it should brown in 40 seconds). Deep-fry the samosas, two or three at a time, for 3–5 minutes or until pale golden. Drain on kitchen paper. Serve warm, garnished with mint and lime.

EASY		NUTRITIONAL INFORMATION		Makes
Preparation Time 45 minutes	**Cooking Time** 15 minutes	**Per Samosa** 136 calories, 6g fat (of which 1g saturates), 19g carbohydrate, 0.3g salt	Vegetarian	**24**

Cook's Tip

About 12 cardamom pods will yield 1 tsp crushed seeds.

Get Ahead

To prepare ahead Deep-fry and drain as step 4.
To use Reheat on a baking sheet at 200°C (180°C fan oven) mark 6 for about 10 minutes before serving.

Onion Bhajis

450g (1lb) onions, halved

1 garlic clove, finely chopped

2.5cm (1in) piece fresh root ginger, peeled and finely chopped

1–2 hot red chillies, peeled, seeded, if you like, and chopped (see page 15)

1 tsp ground turmeric

1 tsp ground cardamom seeds

125g (4oz) gram or plain wholemeal flour, sifted

50g (2oz) self-raising flour

3 tbsp freshly chopped mint

1 tbsp lemon juice

oil for deep-frying

salt and ground black pepper

mint sprigs and lime wedges, to garnish

1 Cut each onion half into very thin slices. Put the onions, garlic, ginger and chillies into a bowl. Add the ground spices and toss well. Add the flours, mint and salt and pepper. Mix thoroughly. Add the lemon juice and about 5 tbsp cold water or enough to make the mixture cling together; do not make it too wet.

2 Heat the oil in a deep-fat fryer. Test by frying a small cube of bread; it should sizzle immediately and rise to the surface. Remove with a slotted spoon.

3 Divide the mixture into 12 portions. Using dampened hands, shape each into a ball. Pat firmly to ensure that it will hold together during cooking.

4 Deep-fry three to four bhajis at a time for 5 minutes or until golden brown on all sides. Carefully remove from the hot oil and drain on crumpled kitchen paper. Serve the bhajis warm, garnished with mint sprigs and lime wedges.

Makes 12	EASY		NUTRITIONAL INFORMATION	
	Preparation Time 20 minutes	**Cooking Time** 15 minutes	**Per Bhaji** 87 calories, 4g fat (of which 0.4g saturates), 11g carbohydrate, 0.3g salt	Vegetarian Dairy free

Cook's Tip

Coriander Chutney Put 1 onion, quartered, in a food processor or blender with 1 garlic clove, 2 hot red chillies, stalks removed, 2 tsp sugar, 1 tsp salt, 2 tbsp lime or lemon juice, 2 tbsp vegetable oil and 1 tbsp ground almonds. Add all but 1 handful of a bunch of fresh coriander. Whiz until well mixed but with some texture. Transfer to a bowl. Chop the reserved coriander and stir into the chutney with 2 canned or bottled red peppers, drained and chopped. Cover and leave to stand for 30 minutes.

2 tsp cumin seeds

2 tsp coriander seeds

1–2 dried red chillies

2 tbsp vegetable oil, plus extra for deep-frying

175g (6oz) gram flour

2 tsp garam masala (see page 11)

1 tsp salt

handful of fresh mint leaves (optional)

550g (1¼lb) prepared vegetables, such as sliced onion, or mushrooms, cauliflower, okra, aubergine, cut into small chunks

Coriander Chutney to serve (see Cook's Tip)

Pakoras

1 Crush the cumin and coriander seeds and dried chillies, using a pestle and mortar. Heat the oil in a frying pan, add the spice mixture and fry for 2 minutes, stirring. Mix the gram flour, garam masala and salt in a bowl. Add the spice mixture, then gradually stir in about 200ml (7fl oz) cold water or enough to make a thick batter. Beat vigorously with a wooden spoon or balloon whisk to remove any lumps. Stir in the whole mint leaves, if using. Leave the batter to stand for about 30 minutes.

2 Heat the oil in a deep-fat fryer to 190°C (375°F) (test by frying a small cube of bread; it should brown in 20 seconds).

3 Fry the vegetables in batches. Dip a few pieces into the batter, then remove one piece at a time and carefully lower into the oil. Cook for 4 minutes or until golden brown. Drain on crumpled kitchen paper. Repeat with the remaining vegetables. Serve with Coriander Chutney.

EASY		NUTRITIONAL INFORMATION		Makes
Preparation Time 40 minutes, plus standing	**Cooking Time** 12–16 minutes	**Per Pakora** 75 calories, 5g fat (of which 1g saturates), 6g carbohydrate, 0.5g salt	Vegetarian Dairy free	**18**

Cook's Tip

If the curds and whey do not separate in step 1, add another 1 tbsp lemon juice and reheat.

Cumin Courgettes with Paneer

3 tbsp oil

125g (4oz) onion, peeled and sliced

900g (2lb) courgettes, sliced into 5mm (¼in) pieces

1 tsp ground turmeric

1 tsp chilli powder

2 tsp white cumin seeds

450g (1lb) tomatoes, peeled and roughly chopped (see page 18)

2 tbsp tomato purée

salt and ground black pepper

For the paneer

2.3 litres (4 pints) full-fat milk

about 5 tbsp strained lemon juice

oil for frying

1 To make the paneer, bring the milk to the boil in a deep pan. As soon as it boils, remove from the heat and add the lemon juice. Stir thoroughly, then return to the heat for about 1 minute; the curds and whey should separate very quickly. Immediately remove the pan from the heat.

2 Line a large sieve or colander with a double thickness of muslin and put over a large bowl. Pour the curds and whey into the muslin and leave until cool enough to handle.

3 Gather up the muslin around the curds and squeeze to remove the excess whey; discard the whey. Put the wrapped curds on a chopping board. Put a small board on top and weight it down with a few large cans or weights. Leave for 3–4 hours until the cheese feels firm.

4 Heat the oil in a large frying pan and fry the onions until well browned. Add the courgettes with the turmeric, chilli powder and cumin seeds. Fry gently for 2–3 minutes, stirring.

5 Add the tomatoes, tomato purée and 150ml (¼ pint) water. Season with salt and pepper. Bring to the boil, cover and simmer for 15–20 minutes or until the courgettes are just tender.

6 Meanwhile, remove the muslin from the paneer and cut into 1cm (½in) cubes. Heat 2.5cm (1in) depth of oil in a deep frying pan and fry the paneer cubes a few at a time without stirring until brown. Drain on kitchen paper.

7 Stir the paneer cubes into the courgette mixture and heat gently for 1–2 minutes. Serve.

Serves	A LITTLE EFFORT		NUTRITIONAL INFORMATION	
6	**Preparation Time** 25 minutes, plus pressing	**Cooking Time** about 30 minutes	**Per Serving** 406 calories, 27g fat (of which 11g saturates), 25g carbohydrate, 0.5g salt	Vegetarian Gluten free

Dal with Aubergine and Mushrooms

350g (12oz) green lentils
1 tsp ground turmeric
2 garlic cloves, crushed
1 aubergine
225g (8oz) mushrooms, wiped and halved
1–2 tsp salt
1/2 tsp sugar
3 tbsp ghee or vegetable oil
1 tsp cumin seeds
1 tsp black mustard seeds
1/2 tsp fennel seeds
1 tsp garam masala (see page 11)
freshly chopped coriander, to garnish

1 Put the lentils into a sieve and wash thoroughly under cold running water. Drain well, then put in a large pan with the turmeric and garlic. Cover with 1.4 litres (2½ pints) water. Boil rapidly for 10 minutes, then simmer for about 20 minutes.

2 Meanwhile, wash the aubergine and pat dry with kitchen paper. Cut into 2.5cm (1in) cubes, discarding the ends.

3 Add the aubergine and mushrooms to the lentil mixture with the salt and sugar. Continue simmering gently for 15–20 minutes until all the vegetables are tender.

4 Heat the ghee or oil in a separate small pan, add the remaining spices and fry for 1 minute or until the mustard seeds begin to pop.

5 Stir the spice mixture into the lentil mixture, cover the pan tightly with the lid and remove from the heat. Leave to stand for 5 minutes, for the flavours to develop. Transfer to a warmed serving dish and garnish with coriander. Serve hot.

EASY		NUTRITIONAL INFORMATION		Serves
Preparation Time 15 minutes	**Cooking Time** 25 minutes, plus standing	**Per Serving** 267 calories, 9g fat (of which 5g saturates), 32g carbohydrate, 0.8g salt	Vegetarian Gluten free • Dairy free	**6**

2

Vegetarian

Curried Coconut and Vegetable Rice

Spiced Egg Pilau

Potato and Broccoli Curry

Vegetable Curry

Tofu Noodle Curry

Chickpea Curry

Thai Vegetable Curry

Mauritian Vegetable Curry

Aubergine and Pepper Balti
with Carrot Relish

Lentil Chilli

Vegetable Korma

Vegetable Biryani

Curried Coconut and Vegetable Rice

1 large aubergine, about 300g (11oz), trimmed

1 large butternut squash, about 500g (1lb 2oz), peeled and seeded

250g (9oz) dwarf green beans, trimmed

100ml (3½fl oz) vegetable oil

1 large onion, chopped

1 tbsp black mustard seeds

3 tbsp korma paste (see page 104)

350g (12oz) basmati rice, rinsed (see page 25)

400ml can coconut milk

200g (7oz) baby spinach leaves

salt and ground black pepper

1 Cut the aubergine and butternut squash into 2cm (¾in) cubes, then slice the green beans into pieces 2cm (¾in) long.

2 Heat the oil in a large pan. Add the onion and cook for about 5 minutes until a light golden colour. Add the mustard seeds and cook, stirring, until they begin to pop. Stir in the korma paste and cook for 1 minute.

3 Add the aubergine and cook, stirring, for 5 minutes. Add the butternut squash, beans, rice and 2 tsp salt, mixing well. Pour in the coconut milk and add 600ml (1 pint) water. Bring to the boil, cover and simmer for 15–18 minutes.

4 When the rice and vegetables are cooked, remove the lid and put the spinach leaves on top. Cover and leave, off the heat, for 5 minutes. Gently stir the wilted spinach through the rice, check the seasoning and serve immediately.

Serves 6	EASY		NUTRITIONAL INFORMATION	
	Preparation Time 15 minutes	**Cooking Time** 30 minutes, plus 5 minutes standing	**Per Serving** 413 calories, 16.8g fat (of which 1.9g saturates), 57.1g carbohydrate, 0.4g salt	Vegetarian Gluten free • Dairy free

Cook's Tip

Coconut cream is sold in cartons, has a thick creamy texture and can be used in sweet and savoury dishes. Creamed coconut is a solid block of coconut, which can be grated or crumbled into sauces to thicken them. It can also be dissolved in hot water to make coconut cream for this recipe: roughly chop 125g (4oz) coconut cream, add 200ml (7fl oz) hot water, leave for 5 minutes, then beat well until smooth.

200g (7oz) basmati or wild rice

150g (5oz) frozen peas

4 medium eggs

200ml (7fl oz) coconut cream (see Cook's Tip)

1 tsp mild curry paste (see Cook's Tip, page 54)

1 tbsp sweet chilli sauce

1 tbsp smooth peanut butter

1 large bunch of fresh coriander, roughly chopped

mini poppadoms and mango chutney to serve

Spiced Egg Pilau

1 Put the rice in a pan with 450ml (¾ pint) boiling water, set over a low heat and cook for 15 minutes or until just tender. Add the peas for the last 5 minutes of cooking time.

2 Meanwhile, put the eggs into a large pan of boiling water and simmer for 6 minutes, then drain and shell.

3 Put the coconut cream, curry paste, chilli sauce and peanut butter into a small pan and whisk together. Heat the sauce gently, stirring, without allowing it to boil.

4 Drain the rice and stir in the chopped coriander and 2 tbsp of the sauce.

5 Divide the rice among four bowls. Cut the eggs into halves and serve on the rice, spooning the remaining coconut sauce over the top. Serve with poppadoms and mango chutney.

EASY		NUTRITIONAL INFORMATION		Serves
Preparation Time 5 minutes	**Cooking Time** 15 minutes	**Per Serving** 331 calories, 9g fat (of which 12g saturates), 50g carbohydrate, 0.6g salt	Vegetarian Gluten free • Dairy free	**4**

Potato and Broccoli Curry

600g (1lb 5oz) new potatoes, scrubbed and cut into bite-size cubes

2 tbsp sunflower oil

2 onions, peeled and sliced

400g can chickpeas, drained and rinsed

250ml (9fl oz) hot vegetable stock (see Cook's Tips)

150g (5oz) broccoli, chopped

salt and ground black pepper

2 tbsp each mango chutney and Greek yogurt, mixed together, and naan bread to serve

For the spice mix

2 tsp ground cumin

2 tsp paprika

1 tsp ground coriander

finely grated zest of ½ orange

1 Cook the potatoes in a pan of lightly salted boiling water for 5 minutes, then drain.

2 Meanwhile, stir the ingredients for the spice mix together with a good pinch of salt. Dry-fry the spice mix for 2–3 minutes in a large frying pan, then add the oil and onions and fry for 7–8 minutes until soft and golden.

3 Add the potatoes, chickpeas and hot stock. Season with salt and pepper, then cook for 15–20 minutes, adding the broccoli for the last 4–5 minutes of cooking time. Serve with the mango chutney, yogurt and naan bread.

Cook's Tips

You could use any canned pulses in this curry, such as butter beans, black-eyed peas or brown lentils.

You can use 1 vegetable stock cube dissolved in 250ml (9fl oz) boiling water.

EASY		NUTRITIONAL INFORMATION		Serves
Preparation Time 20 minutes	**Cooking Time** 40 minutes	**Per Serving** 302 calories, 10g fat (of which 1g saturates), 46g carbohydrate, 0.5g salt	Vegetarian Gluten free	**4**

Cook's Tip

Check the ingredients in the curry paste; some contain shrimp and are therefore not suitable for vegetarians.

Vegetable Curry

1 tbsp medium curry paste (see Cook's Tip)

227g can chopped tomatoes

150ml (¼ pint) hot vegetable stock

200g (7oz) vegetables, such as broccoli, courgettes and sugarsnap peas, roughly chopped

½ x 400g can chickpeas, drained and rinsed

griddled wholemeal pitta bread and yogurt to serve

1 Heat the curry paste in a large heavy-based pan for 1 minute, stirring the paste to warm the spices. Add the tomatoes and hot stock. Bring to the boil, then reduce the heat to a simmer and add the vegetables. Simmer for 5–6 minutes until the vegetables are just tender.

2 Stir in the chickpeas and heat for 1–2 minutes until hot. Serve the vegetable curry with a griddled wholemeal pitta and yogurt.

Serves	EASY		NUTRITIONAL INFORMATION	
1	**Preparation Time** 5 minutes	**Cooking Time** 12 minutes	**Per Serving** 468 calories, 20g fat of which 3g saturates), 58g carbohydrate, 1.4g salt	Vegetarian Gluten free • Dairy free

Tofu Noodle Curry

250g (9oz) fresh tofu

2 tbsp light soy sauce

½ red chilli, chopped (see page 15)

5cm (2in) piece fresh root ginger, peeled and grated

1 tbsp olive oil

1 onion, finely sliced

2 tbsp Thai red curry paste (see Cook's Tip, page 54)

200ml (7fl oz) coconut milk

900ml (1½ pints) hot vegetable stock

200g (7oz) baby sweetcorn, halved

200g (7oz) fine green beans, trimmed and halved

250g (9oz) medium rice noodles

salt and ground black pepper

2 spring onions, sliced diagonally, and 2 tbsp fresh coriander leaves to garnish

1 lime, cut into wedges, to serve

1 Drain the tofu, pat it dry and cut it into large cubes. Put the tofu into a shallow dish with the soy sauce, chilli and ginger. Toss to coat, then leave to marinate for 30 minutes.

2 Heat the oil in a large pan over a medium heat, then add the onion and fry for 10 minutes, stirring, until golden. Add the curry paste and cook for 2 minutes.

3 Add the tofu and marinade, coconut milk, hot stock and sweetcorn, and season with salt and pepper. Bring to the boil, add the green beans, then reduce the heat and simmer for 8–10 minutes.

4 Meanwhile, put the noodles into a large bowl, pour boiling water over them and soak for 30 seconds. Drain the noodles, then stir into the curry. Pour into bowls and garnish with the spring onions and coriander. Serve immediately, with lime wedges.

EASY		NUTRITIONAL INFORMATION		Serves
Preparation Time 15 minutes, plus marinating	**Cooking Time** about 25 minutes	**Per Serving** 367 calories, 7g fat (of which 1g saturates), 60g carbohydrate, 2g salt	Vegetarian Dairy free	**4**

Chickpea Curry

2 tbsp vegetable oil

2 onions, finely sliced

2 garlic cloves, crushed

1 tbsp ground coriander

1 tsp mild chilli powder

1 tbsp black mustard seeds

2 tbsp tamarind paste

2 tbsp sun-dried tomato paste

750g (1lb 10oz) new potatoes, quartered

400g can chopped tomatoes

1 litre (1³/₄ pints) hot vegetable stock

250g (9oz) green beans, trimmed and halved

2 x 400g cans chickpeas, drained and rinsed

2 tsp garam masala (see page 11)

salt and ground black pepper

1 Heat the oil in a pan and fry the sliced onions for 10–15 minutes until golden – when they have a good colour they will add depth of flavour. Add the garlic, coriander, chilli, mustard seeds, tamarind paste and sun-dried tomato paste. Cook for 1–2 minutes until the aroma from the spices is released.

2 Add the potatoes and toss in the spice mixture for 1–2 minutes. Add the tomatoes and hot stock, and season with salt and pepper. Cover and bring to the boil, then reduce the heat and simmer, half covered, for 20 minutes or until the potatoes are just cooked.

3 Add the beans and chickpeas, and continue to cook for 5 minutes or until the beans are tender and the chickpeas are warmed through. Stir in the garam masala and serve.

Serves	EASY		NUTRITIONAL INFORMATION	
6	**Preparation Time** 20 minutes	**Cooking Time** 40–45 minutes	**Per Serving** 291 calories, 8g fat (of which 1g saturates), 46g carbohydrate, 1.3g salt	Vegetarian Gluten free • Dairy free

Try Something Different

Replace the carrots and/or broccoli with alternative vegetables – try baby sweetcorn, sugarsnap peas or mangetouts and simmer for only 5 minutes until tender.

Thai Vegetable Curry

2–3 tbsp red Thai curry paste (see Cook's Tip, page 54)

2.5cm (1in) piece fresh root ginger, peeled and finely chopped

50g (2oz) cashew nuts

400ml can coconut milk

3 carrots, cut into thin batons

1 broccoli head, cut into florets

20g (¾ oz) fresh coriander, roughly chopped

zest and juice of 1 lime

2 large handfuls of spinach leaves

basmati rice to serve

1 Put the curry paste into a large pan, add the ginger and cashew nuts and stir-fry over a medium heat for 2–3 minutes.

2 Add the coconut milk, cover the pan and bring to the boil. Stir the carrots into the pan, then reduce the heat and simmer for 5 minutes. Add the broccoli florets and simmer for a further 5 minutes until just tender.

3 Stir the coriander and lime zest into the pan with the spinach. Squeeze the lime juice over and serve with basmati rice.

Serves 4	EASY		NUTRITIONAL INFORMATION	
	Preparation Time 10 minutes	**Cooking Time** 15 minutes	**Per Serving** 200 calories, 10g fat (of which 2g saturates), 19g carbohydrate, 0.7g salt	Vegetarian Gluten free • Dairy free

Get Ahead

To prepare ahead, Complete the recipe, without the garnish, and chill quickly. It will keep in the fridge for up to two days.

To use Put into a pan, cover and bring to the boil, then simmer for 10–15 minutes. Complete the recipe.

Mauritian Vegetable Curry

1 Heat the oil in a large heavy-based pan over a low heat. Add the onion and fry for 5–10 minutes until golden. Add the garlic, ginger, curry powder and curry leaves, and fry for a further minute.

2 Add the potato and aubergine to the pan and fry, stirring, for 2 minutes. Add the carrots, hot stock, saffron and salt, and season with plenty of pepper. Cover and cook for 10 minutes or until the vegetables are almost tender.

3 Add the beans and peas to the pan and cook for a further 4 minutes. Sprinkle with the chopped coriander and serve with pitta bread.

3 tbsp vegetable oil

1 onion, finely sliced

4 garlic cloves, crushed

2.5cm (1in) piece fresh root ginger, peeled and grated

3 tbsp medium curry powder

6 fresh curry leaves

150g (5oz) potatoes, cut into 1cm (½in) cubes

125g (4oz) aubergine, cut into 2cm (¾in) sticks, 5mm (¼in) wide

150g (5oz) carrots, cut into 5mm (¼in) dice

900ml (1½ pints) hot vegetable stock

a pinch of saffron threads

1 tsp salt

150g (5oz) green beans, trimmed

75g (3oz) frozen peas

ground black pepper

3 tbsp freshly chopped coriander to garnish

pitta bread to serve

EASY		NUTRITIONAL INFORMATION		Serves
Preparation Time 15 minutes	**Cooking Time** 30 minutes	**Per Serving** 184 calories, 11g fat (of which 1g saturates), 18g carbohydrate, 1.7g salt	Vegetarian Gluten free • Dairy free	4

Cook's Tip

Balti paste Put 1 tbsp each fennel seeds and ground allspice into a food processor with 2–3 chopped garlic cloves, 1cm (1/2in) piece fresh root ginger, peeled and chopped, 50g (2oz) garam masala, 25g (1oz) curry powder and 1 tsp salt. Add 8 tbsp water and blend. Divide the paste into three portions, use one and freeze two (see page 74).

Aubergine and Pepper Balti with Carrot Relish

4 tbsp groundnut oil, plus 1 tsp for the relish

1 onion, finely sliced

1 aubergine, cut into 2cm (³/₄in) dice

balti paste (see Cook's Tip)

1 red and 1 green chilli, seeded and roughly chopped (see page 15)

1 red and 1 green pepper, seeded and sliced

4 tomatoes, about 300g (11oz), quartered

600ml (1 pint) vegetable stock

2 tsp black mustard seeds

450g (1lb) carrots, grated

2 tbsp tamarind paste

2 tbsp dark muscovado sugar

1 tbsp white wine vinegar

50g (2oz) baby spinach leaves

salt and ground black pepper

pilau rice to serve

1 To make the curry, heat 4 tbsp oil in a large flameproof casserole and fry the onion over a high heat for 10–15 minutes until golden. Add the aubergine and cook for another 5 minutes.

2 Add the balti paste and the chillies to the casserole, stir well to mix and cook for 1–2 minutes. Add the peppers and tomatoes and cook for 5 minutes, then add the stock and season well. Cover and bring to the boil, then reduce the heat and simmer the balti for 15 minutes or until the vegetables are tender.

3 Meanwhile, make the carrot relish. Heat the 1 tsp oil in a pan and add the mustard seeds. Cover with a lid and cook until they start to pop – you'll hear them jumping against the lid. Add the carrots, tamarind paste, sugar and vinegar to the pan and cook for 1–2 minutes. Stir well.

4 Stir the spinach into the curry and serve with the carrot relish and pilau rice to soak up the sauce.

Serves 4	EASY		NUTRITIONAL INFORMATION	
	Preparation Time 30 minutes	**Cooking Time** 45 minutes	**Per Serving** 364 calories, 17.6g fat (of which 2g saturates), 46.5g carbohydrate, 0.4g salt	Vegetarian Gluten free • Dairy free

Cook's Tip

Oil-water spray is far lower in calories than oil alone and, as it sprays on thinly and evenly, you'll use less. Fill one-eighth of a travel-sized spray bottle with oil such as sunflower, light olive or vegetable (rapeseed) oil, then top up with water. To use, shake well before spraying. Store in the fridge.

Lentil Chilli

oil-water spray (see Cook's Tip)

2 red onions, chopped

1½ tsp each ground coriander and ground cumin

½ tsp ground paprika

2 garlic cloves, crushed

2 sun-dried tomatoes, chopped

¼ tsp dried chilli flakes

125ml (4fl oz) red wine

300ml (½ pint) vegetable stock

2 x 400g cans brown or green lentils, drained and rinsed

2 x 400g cans chopped tomatoes

sugar to taste

salt and ground black pepper

natural low-fat yogurt and rice to serve

1 Spray a large pan with the oil-water spray, add the onions and cook for 5 minutes until softened. Add the coriander, cumin and paprika. Combine the garlic, sun-dried tomatoes, chilli flakes, wine and stock and add to the pan. Cover and simmer for 5–7 minutes. Uncover and simmer until the onions are very tender and the liquid has almost gone.

2 Stir in the lentils and tomatoes and season with salt and pepper. Simmer, uncovered, for 15 minutes until thick. Stir in sugar to taste. Remove from the heat.

3 Ladle out a quarter of the mixture and blend in a food processor or blender. Combine the puréed and unpuréed portions. Serve with yogurt and rice.

EASY		NUTRITIONAL INFORMATION		Serves
Preparation Time 10 minutes	**Cooking Time** 30 minutes	**Per Serving** 191 calories, 2g fat (of which trace saturates), 30g carbohydrate, 0g salt	Vegetarian Gluten free • Dairy free	**6**

Vegetable Korma

2 tbsp ghee or vegetable oil

1 large onion, chopped

1–2 garlic cloves, crushed

2.5cm (1in) piece fresh root ginger, peeled and chopped

1 tbsp coriander seeds

1 tsp whole cloves

2 tsp black peppercorns

6 green cardamoms

900g (2lb) mixed prepared vegetables, including some root vegetables, cut into chunks

2 tsp ground turmeric

finely grated rind and juice of $\frac{1}{2}$ lime or lemon

50g (2oz) ground almonds

200ml (7fl oz) double cream

salt

50g (2oz) flaked almonds

3 tbsp freshly chopped coriander (optional)

1 Heat the ghee or oil in a large, heavy-based pan. Add the onion, garlic and ginger and fry very gently, stirring frequently, for 10 minutes or until soft and lightly coloured.

2 Meanwhile, finely grind the whole spices and peppercorns in an electric grinder or by hand using a pestle and mortar. Add to the pan and fry for 2 minutes, stirring all the time. Increase the heat, add the vegetables and turmeric and fry for 1–2 minutes. Add the lime or lemon rind and juice, the ground almonds and 300ml ($\frac{1}{2}$ pint) water. Cover and simmer for 30–40 minutes or until the vegetables are just tender (the time will depend upon the type of vegetables used).

3 Slowly stir in the cream and a little water if the korma is too dry. Season with salt and cook gently until heated through. Transfer to a warmed serving dish, sprinkle with the almonds and coriander, if using, and serve immediately.

EASY		NUTRITIONAL INFORMATION		Serves
Preparation Time 20 minutes	**Cooking Time** 50 minutes	**Per Serving** 339 calories, 28g fat (of which 15g saturates), 16g carbohydrate, 0.5g salt	Vegetarian Gluten free	**6**

Vegetable Biryani

350g (12oz) basmati rice, rinsed
(see page 25)

50g (2oz) ghee or oil

1 large onion, chopped

2.5cm (1in) piece fresh root ginger, peeled and grated

1–2 garlic cloves, crushed

1 tsp ground coriander

2 tsp ground cumin

1 tsp ground turmeric

1/2 tsp chilli powder

3 carrots, thinly sliced

225g (8oz) French beans, trimmed and halved

225g (8oz) small cauliflower florets

1 tsp garam masala (see page 11)

juice of 1 lemon

salt and ground black pepper

hard-boiled egg slices and fresh coriander sprigs,
to garnish

1 Put the rice in a pan with 600ml (1 pint) water and 1 tsp salt. Bring to the boil, then reduce the heat and simmer for 10 minutes or until only just tender.

2 Meanwhile, heat the ghee or oil in a large heavy-based pan, add the onion, ginger and garlic and fry gently for 5 minutes or until soft but not coloured. Add the coriander, cumin, turmeric and chilli powder and fry for 2 minutes more, stirring constantly to prevent the spices catching and burning.

3 Remove the rice from the heat and drain. Add 900ml (1 1/2 pints) water to the onion and spice mixture and season with salt and pepper. Stir well and bring to the boil. Add the carrots and beans and simmer for 15 minutes, then add the cauliflower and simmer for a further 10 minutes. Lastly, add the rice. Fold gently to mix and simmer until reheated.

4 Stir the garam masala and lemon juice into the biryani and simmer for a few minutes more to reheat and allow the flavours to develop. Taste and adjust the seasoning, if necessary, then turn into a warmed serving dish. Garnish with egg slices and coriander sprigs and serve immediately.

Serves	EASY		NUTRITIONAL INFORMATION	
4	**Preparation Time** 20 minutes	**Cooking Time** 45 minutes	**Per Serving** 507 calories, 14g fat (of which 8g saturates), 84g carbohydrate, 0.7g salt	Vegetarian Gluten free • Dairy free

Poultry

Chicken Tikka with Coconut Dressing

Caribbean Chicken

Fiery Mango Chicken

Tandoori Chicken with Cucumber Raita

Mild Spiced Chicken with Quinoa

Spiced Chicken Pilau

Chicken Tikka Masala

Morrocan Chicken with Chickpeas

Chicken, Bean and Spinach Curry

Hot Jungle Curry

Easy Thai Red Chicken Curry

Thai Green Curry

Turkey Curry

Crispy Duck with Hot and Sweet Dip

Chicken Dhansak

Chicken Tikka with Coconut Dressing

125ml (4fl oz) crème fraîche

5 tbsp coconut milk

4 pitta breads

200g (7oz) mixed salad leaves

400g (14oz) cooked chicken tikka fillets, sliced

2 spring onions, finely sliced

2 tbsp mango chutney

15g (½oz) flaked almonds

25g (1oz) raisins

1 Mix the crème fraîche and coconut milk together in a bowl and put to one side.

2 Split each pitta bread to form a pocket, then fill with a generous handful of salad leaves. Divide the chicken among the pitta breads. Sprinkle some spring onion over the chicken, add the mango chutney and drizzle with the crème fraîche mixture. Top with a sprinkling of flaked almonds and raisins. Serve immediately.

EASY	NUTRITIONAL INFORMATION	Serves
Preparation Time 10 minutes	**Per Serving** 503 calories, 19.1g fat (of which 9.9g saturates), 55.2g carbohydrate, 1.3g salt	**4**

Cook's Tip

Scotch bonnets are small but very hot green, yellow or red chillies frequently used in Caribbean cooking.

Caribbean Chicken

10 chicken pieces, such as thighs, drumsticks, wings or breasts, skinned and pierced with a knife

1 tbsp ground coriander

2 tsp ground cumin

1 tbsp paprika

pinch of ground nutmeg

1 fresh Scotch bonnet (see Cook's Tip) or other hot red chilli, seeded and chopped (see page 15)

1 onion, chopped

5 fresh thyme sprigs, plus extra to garnish

4 garlic cloves, crushed

2 tbsp dark soy sauce

juice of 1 lemon

2 tbsp vegetable oil

2 tbsp light muscovado sugar

350g (12oz) American easy-cook rice

3 tbsp dark rum (optional)

25g (1oz) butter

2 x 300g cans black-eyed beans, drained and rinsed

salt and ground black pepper

1 Sprinkle the chicken with ½ tsp salt, some pepper, the coriander, cumin, paprika and nutmeg. Add the chilli, onion, thyme and garlic, then pour the soy sauce and lemon juice over the chicken and stir to combine. Cover and chill for at least 4 hours.

2 Heat a 3.4 litre (6 pint) heavy-based pan over a medium heat for 2 minutes. Add the oil and sugar and cook for 3 minutes or until it turns a rich golden caramel colour. (Be careful not to overcook it as it will blacken and taste burnt – watch it very closely.)

3 Remove the chicken pieces from the marinade and add to the caramel mixture in the hot pan. Cover and cook over a medium heat for 5 minutes, then turn the chicken and cook, covered, for another 5 minutes until evenly browned. Add the reserved marinade. Turn the chicken again, then cover and cook for 10 minutes.

4 Add the rice, stir to combine, then pour in 900ml (1½ pints) cold water. Add the rum, if using, the butter and ½ tsp salt. Cover and simmer, without lifting the lid, for 20 minutes or until the rice is tender and most of the liquid has been absorbed.

5 Add the black-eyed beans and mix well. Cover and cook for 3–5 minutes until the beans are warmed through and all the liquid has been absorbed, taking care that the rice doesn't stick to the bottom of the pan. Garnish with fresh thyme and serve hot.

Serves 5	EASY		NUTRITIONAL INFORMATION	
	Preparation Time 40 minutes, plus marinating	**Cooking Time** 45–50 minutes	**Per Serving** 617 calories, 39g fat (of which 12g saturates), 25g carbohydrate, 2.1g salt	Gluten free

Fiery Mango Chicken

4 tbsp hot mango chutney (or ordinary mango chutney, plus ½ tsp Tabasco)

grated zest and juice of 1 lime

4 tbsp natural yogurt

2 tbsp freshly chopped coriander, plus extra sprigs to garnish

1 small green chilli (optional), seeded and finely chopped (see page 15)

4 chicken breasts with skin on

1 large ripe mango, peeled and stoned

oil to brush

salt and ground black pepper

lime wedges and rice to serve

1 In a large shallow dish, mix together the chutney, lime zest and juice, yogurt, chopped coriander and, if you would like the dish to be hot and spicy, the chilli.

2 Put the chicken breasts, skin side-down, on the worksurface, cover with clingfilm and beat lightly with a rolling pin. Slice each into three pieces, then put into the yogurt mixture and stir to coat. Cover and chill for at least 30 minutes or overnight.

3 Preheat the barbecue or grill. Slice the mango into four thick pieces. Brush lightly with oil and season well with salt and pepper. Barbecue or grill for about 2 minutes on each side – the fruit should be lightly charred but still firm. Put to one side.

4 Barbecue or grill the chicken for 3–5 minutes on each side until golden. Garnish with coriander and serve with the grilled mango, lime wedges and rice.

EASY		NUTRITIONAL INFORMATION		Serves
Preparation Time 15 minutes, plus marinating	**Cooking Time** 10 minutes	**Per Serving** 297 calories, 14.1g fat (of which 4.1g saturates), 7.8g carbohydrate, 0.3g salt	Gluten free	**4**

Tandoori Chicken with Cucumber Raita

4 tbsp groundnut oil, plus extra to grease

3 x 150g cartons natural yogurt

juice of ½ lemon

4 skinless chicken breasts, about 600g (1lb 5oz), cut into finger-width pieces

½ cucumber

salt and ground black pepper

mint leaves to garnish

For the tandoori paste

24 garlic cloves, about 125g (4oz), crushed

5cm (2in) piece fresh root ginger, peeled and chopped

3 tbsp each coriander seeds, cumin seeds, ground fenugreek and paprika

3 red chillies, seeded and chopped (see page 15)

3 tsp English mustard

2 tbsp tomato purée

1 tsp salt

1 Put all the ingredients for the tandoori paste into a food processor with 8 tbsp water and blend to a paste. Divide the paste into three equal portions, freeze two (see Freezing Tips) and put the other in a large bowl.

2 To make the tandoori chicken, add 1 tbsp oil, 2 cartons of yogurt and the lemon juice to the paste. Add the chicken and stir well to coat. Cover the bowl, chill and marinate the chicken for at least 4 hours.

3 Preheat the oven to 220°C (200°C fan oven) mark 7. Oil a roasting tin. Put the chicken in it, drizzle the remaining oil over the chicken and roast for 20 minutes or until cooked through.

4 Meanwhile, prepare the raita. Whisk the remaining carton of yogurt. Using a vegetable peeler, scrape the cucumber into very thin strips. Put the strips in a bowl and pour the whisked yogurt over them. Season, then chill until ready to serve. Garnish the cucumber raita with mint leaves. Sprinkle the chicken with mint and serve with the raita.

Freezing Tips

At the end of step 1, put two of the portions of tandoori paste into separate freezer bags and freeze. They will keep for up to three months.

To use the frozen paste, put the paste in a microwave and cook on Defrost for 1 minute 20 seconds (based on 900W oven), or thaw at a cool room temperature for 1 hour.

Serves 4	EASY		NUTRITIONAL INFORMATION	
	Preparation Time 45 minutes, plus marinating	**Cooking Time** 20 minutes	**Per Serving** 399 calories, 19.9g fat (of which 3.5g saturates), 14.9g carbohydrate, 1.8g salt	Gluten free

Cook's Tip

Quinoa is a grain, first grown by the Incas, that can be used in place of rice. It has a mild flavour and slightly chewy texture.

Mild Spiced Chicken with Quinoa

2 tbsp mango chutney

juice of 1/2 lemon

1 tbsp olive oil

2 tsp mild curry powder

1 tsp paprika

350g (12oz) skinless chicken breast, cut into thick strips

200g (7oz) quinoa (see Cook's Tip)

1 cucumber, roughly chopped

1/2 bunch of spring onions, sliced

50g (2oz) ready-to-eat dried apricots, sliced

2 tbsp freshly chopped mint, basil or tarragon

salt and ground black pepper

mint leaves to garnish

1 Put the chutney, lemon juice, 1/2 tbsp oil, the curry powder and paprika into a bowl and mix together. Add the chicken and toss to coat.

2 Cook the quinoa in boiling water for 10–12 minutes until tender, or according to the pack instructions. Drain thoroughly. Put into a bowl, then stir in the cucumber, spring onions, apricots, herbs and remaining oil. Season with salt and pepper.

3 Meanwhile, put the chicken and marinade into a pan and fry over a high heat for 2–3 minutes, then add 150ml (1/4 pint) water. Bring to the boil, then simmer for 5 minutes or until the chicken is cooked. Serve with the quinoa and garnish with mint leaves.

Serves 4	EASY		NUTRITIONAL INFORMATION	
	Preparation Time 15 minutes	**Cooking Time** 10–12 minutes	**Per Serving** 268 calories, 3g fat (of which trace saturates), 37g carbohydrate, 0.4g salt	Gluten free Dairy free

Cook's Tip

This is also a good way to use leftover roast turkey.

Spiced Chicken Pilau

50g (2oz) pinenuts

2 tbsp olive oil

2 onions, sliced

2 garlic cloves, crushed

2 tbsp medium curry powder

6 boneless, skinless chicken thighs or 450g (1lb) skinless cooked chicken, cut into strips

350g (12oz) American easy-cook rice

2 tsp salt

pinch of saffron threads

50g (2oz) sultanas

225g (8oz) ripe tomatoes, roughly chopped

1 Spread the pinenuts over a baking sheet and toast under a hot grill until golden brown, turning them frequently. Put to one side.

2 Heat the oil in a large heavy-based pan over a medium heat. Add the onions and garlic and cook for 5 minutes until soft. Remove half the onion mixture and put to one side.

3 Add the curry powder and cook for 1 minute, then add the chicken and stir. Cook for 10 minutes if the meat is raw, or for 4 minutes if you're using cooked chicken, stirring from time to time until browned.

4 Add the rice, stir to coat in the oil, then add 900ml (1½ pints) boiling water, the salt and saffron. Cover and bring to the boil. Reduce the heat to low and cook for 20 minutes or until the rice is tender and most of the liquid has been absorbed. Stir in the reserved onion mixture, the sultanas, tomatoes and pinenuts. Cook for 5 minutes to warm through, then serve.

EASY		NUTRITIONAL INFORMATION		Serves
Preparation Time 15 minutes	**Cooking Time** 35–40 minutes	**Per Serving** 649 calories, 18g fat (of which 2g saturates), 87g carbohydrate, 2.8g salt	Gluten free Dairy free	**4**

Chicken Tikka Masala

2 tbsp vegetable oil
1 onion, finely sliced
2 garlic cloves, crushed
6 boneless, skinless chicken thighs, cut into strips
2 tbsp tikka masala curry paste
200g can chopped tomatoes
450ml (³/₄ pint) hot vegetable stock
225g (8oz) baby spinach leaves
fresh coriander leaves to garnish
plain boiled rice, mango chutney and poppadoms to serve

1 Heat the oil in a large pan, add the onion and fry over a medium heat for 5–7 minutes until golden. Add the garlic and chicken and stir-fry for about 5 minutes or until golden.

2 Stir in the curry paste, then add the tomatoes and hot stock. Bring to the boil, then reduce the heat, cover the pan and simmer over a low heat for 15 minutes or until the chicken is cooked through.

3 Add the spinach to the curry, stir and cook until the leaves have just wilted. Garnish with coriander and serve with plain boiled rice, mango chutney and poppadoms.

EASY		NUTRITIONAL INFORMATION		Serves
Preparation Time 15 minutes	**Cooking Time** 30 minutes	**Per Serving** 297 calories, 17g fat (of which 4g saturates), 4g carbohydrate, 0.6g salt	Gluten free Dairy free	**4**

Get Ahead

To prepare ahead Complete the recipe, then cool quickly. Put into a sealable container and freeze for up to three months.
To use Thaw overnight in the fridge. Put into a pan, cover and bring to the boil. Reduce the heat to low, then reheat for 40 minutes or until the chicken is hot right through.

Moroccan Chicken with Chickpeas

12 chicken pieces, including thighs, drumsticks and breast, skin on

25g (1oz) butter

1 large onion, sliced

2 garlic cloves, crushed

2 tbsp harissa paste

a generous pinch of saffron

1 tsp salt

1 cinnamon stick

600ml (1 pint) chicken stock

75g (3oz) raisins

2 x 400g cans chickpeas, drained and rinsed

ground black pepper

plain naan or pitta bread to serve

1 Heat a large wide non-stick pan. Add the chicken pieces and fry until well browned all over. Add the butter and, when melted, add the onion and garlic. Cook, stirring, for 5 minutes.

2 Add the harissa, saffron, salt and cinnamon stick, then season well with pepper. Pour in the stock and bring to the boil. Reduce the heat, cover and simmer gently for 25–30 minutes.

3 Add the raisins and chickpeas, and bring to the boil, then reduce the heat and simmer uncovered for 5–10 minutes.

4 Serve with warm flat bread such as plain naan or pitta bread.

Serves 6	EASY		NUTRITIONAL INFORMATION	
	Preparation Time 10 minutes	**Cooking Time** 50 minutes	**Per Serving** 440 calories, 18g fat (of which 6g saturates), 33g carbohydrate, 1g salt	Gluten free

Try Something Different

Instead of chicken, use pork escalopes, cut into thin strips.

Chicken, Bean and Spinach Curry

1 tbsp sunflower oil

350g (12oz) skinless, boneless chicken breasts, cut into strips

1 garlic clove, crushed

300–350g tub or jar curry sauce

400g can aduki beans, drained and rinsed

175g (6oz) ready-to-eat dried apricots

150g (5oz) natural bio yogurt, plus extra to serve

125g (4oz) baby spinach leaves

naan bread to serve

1 Heat the oil in a large pan over a medium heat and fry the chicken strips with the garlic until golden. Add the curry sauce, beans and apricots, then cover and simmer gently for 15 minutes or until the chicken is tender.

2 Over a low heat, stir in the yogurt, keeping the curry hot without boiling it, then stir in the spinach until it just begins to wilt. Add a spoonful of yogurt and serve with naan bread.

EASY		NUTRITIONAL INFORMATION		Serves
Preparation Time 10 minutes	**Cooking Time** 20 minutes	**Per Serving** 358 calories, 10.6g fat (of which 1.5g saturates), 38g carbohydrate, 2.9g salt	Gluten free	**4**

Try Something Different

Add a drained 225g can of bamboo shoots with the other vegetables in step 2, if you like.

Hot Jungle Curry

1 tbsp vegetable oil

350g (12oz) skinless, boneless chicken breasts, cut into 5cm (2in) strips

2 tbsp Thai red curry paste

2.5cm (1in) piece fresh root ginger, peeled and thinly sliced

125g (4oz) aubergine, cut into bite-size pieces

125g (4oz) baby sweetcorn, halved lengthways

75g (3oz) green beans, trimmed

75g (3oz) button or brown-cap mushrooms, halved if large

2–3 kaffir lime leaves (optional)

450ml (¾ pint) chicken stock

2 tbsp Thai fish sauce (nam pla)

grated zest of ½ lime, plus extra to garnish

1 tsp tomato purée

1 tbsp soft brown sugar

1 Heat the oil in a wok or large frying pan. Add the chicken and cook, stirring, for 5 minutes or until the chicken turns golden brown.

2 Add the red curry paste and cook for a further 1 minute. Add the ginger, aubergine, sweetcorn, beans, mushrooms and lime leaves, if using, and stir until coated in the red curry paste. Add all the remaining ingredients and bring to the boil. Reduce the heat and simmer gently for 10–12 minutes until the chicken and vegetables are just tender. Serve immediately, sprinkled with lime zest.

Serves 4	EASY		NUTRITIONAL INFORMATION	
	Preparation Time 10 minutes	**Cooking Time** 18–20 minutes	**Per Serving** 160 calories, 5g fat (of which 1g saturates), 5g carbohydrate, 1.1g salt	Gluten free Dairy free

Easy Thai Red Chicken Curry

1 tbsp vegetable oil

3 tbsp Thai red curry paste

4 boneless, skinless chicken breasts, about 600g (1lb 5oz), sliced

400ml can coconut milk

300ml (½ pint) hot chicken or vegetable stock

juice of 1 lime

200g pack mixed baby sweetcorn and mangetouts

2 tbsp freshly chopped coriander, plus extra leaves to garnish

rice or rice noodles to serve

1 Heat the oil in a wok or large pan over a low heat. Add the curry paste and cook for 2 minutes or until fragrant.

2 Add the sliced chicken and fry gently for about 10 minutes or until browned.

3 Add the coconut milk, hot stock, lime juice and baby corn to the pan and bring to the boil. Add the mangetouts, reduce the heat and simmer for 4–5 minutes until the chicken is cooked. Add the chopped coriander and serve immediately, garnished with coriander leaves, with rice or noodles.

Serves 4	EASY		NUTRITIONAL INFORMATION	
	Preparation Time 5 minutes	**Cooking Time** 20 minutes	**Per Serving** 248 calories, 8g fat (of which 1g saturates), 16g carbohydrate, 1g salt	Gluten free Dairy free

2 tsp vegetable oil

1 green chilli, seeded and finely chopped
(see page 15)

4cm (1½in) piece fresh root ginger,
peeled and finely grated

1 lemongrass stalk, trimmed and cut into three pieces

225g (8oz) brown-cap or oyster mushrooms

1 tbsp Thai green curry paste

300ml (½ pint) coconut milk

150ml (¼ pint) chicken stock

1 tbsp Thai fish sauce (nam pla)

1 tsp light soy sauce

350g (12oz) skinless, boneless chicken breasts,
cut into bite-size pieces

350g (12oz) cooked peeled large prawns

fresh coriander sprigs to garnish

Thai fragrant rice to serve

Thai Green Curry

1 Heat the oil in a wok or large frying pan, add the chilli, ginger, lemongrass and mushrooms, and stir-fry for about 3 minutes or until the mushrooms begin to turn golden. Add the curry paste and fry for a further 1 minute.

2 Pour in the coconut milk, stock, fish sauce and soy sauce and bring to the boil. Stir in the chicken, then reduce the heat and simmer for about 8 minutes or until the chicken is cooked.

3 Add the prawns and cook for a further 1 minute. Garnish with coriander sprigs and serve immediately, with Thai fragrant rice.

EASY		NUTRITIONAL INFORMATION		Serves
Preparation Time 10 minutes	**Cooking Time** 15 minutes	**Per Serving** 132 calories, 2g fat (of which 0g saturates), 4g carbohydrate, 1.4g salt	Dairy free Gluten free	**6**

Try Something Different

- -

For a more intense flavour, fry 1 tsp black mustard seeds with the spices.

Scatter over 2–3 tbsp chopped coriander to serve.

Cook's Tip

- -

This is an ideal recipe for using up turkey leftover from your Christmas meal.

2 tbsp oil

1 large onion, chopped

2 garlic cloves, finely chopped

1 tsp ground turmeric

½ tsp chilli powder

1½ tsp ground cumin

1½ tsp ground coriander

400g can chopped tomatoes

½ tsp salt

600g (1lb 5oz) cooked turkey

1 tsp garam masala (see page 11)

150ml (¼ pint) thick yogurt

coriander to garnish

rice to serve

Turkey Curry

1 Heat the oil in a heavy-based pan, add the onion and garlic, and fry gently until softened and golden. Add the turmeric, chilli powder, cumin and coriander, and cook, stirring, for 1 minute.

2 Add the tomatoes and salt. Bring to the boil, cover and simmer for 20 minutes.

3 Remove any skin from the turkey, then cut into chunks. Add to the pan with the garam masala and 4 tbsp yogurt. Cover and cook gently for 10 minutes, then stir in the remaining yogurt. Garnish with coriander and serve with rice.

Serves	EASY		NUTRITIONAL INFORMATION	
4	Preparation Time 15 minutes	Cooking Time 35 minutes	Per Serving 330 calories 12g fat (of which 4g saturates) 8g carbohydrate 0.4g salt	Gluten free

Crispy Duck with Hot and Sweet Dip

8 small duck legs

2 pieces star anise

4 fat garlic cloves, sliced

1 dried red chilli

grated zest and juice of 1 orange

1 tbsp tamarind juice or lemon juice

fried garlic slivers, fried chilli pieces and star anise to garnish

For the hot and sweet dip

200ml (7fl oz) white wine vinegar

150g (5oz) golden caster sugar

75g (3oz) each cucumber, spring onion and mango, cut into fine shreds

1 dried red chilli or ¼ tsp seeded and shredded red chilli (see page 15)

 1 To make the hot and sweet dip, boil the vinegar and sugar together in a pan for 2 minutes, then stir in the cucumber, spring onion, mango and chilli. Transfer to a serving bowl and leave to cool.

2 Prick the duck legs all over with a skewer or fork. Put them in a large pan, cover with cold water and bring to the boil, then reduce the heat and simmer for 45 minutes.

3 Meanwhile, put the 2 star anise, garlic, chilli, orange zest and juice, and tamarind or lemon juice in a blender and mix to a paste. Preheat the grill.

4 Drain the duck and put, skin-side down, on a foil-lined grill pan. Brush half the spice paste over the duck. Grill for 5 minutes, then turn skin-side up and brush the remaining paste over it. Grill for a further 5–7 minutes or until the duck skin is well charred and crisp. Garnish with the fried garlic slivers, fried chilli pieces and star anise and serve with the hot and sweet dip.

EASY		NUTRITIONAL INFORMATION		Serves
Preparation Time 10 minutes	**Cooking Time** 1 hour	**Per Serving** 504 calories, 28.4g fat (of which 6.3g saturates), 42.4g carbohydrate, 0.5g salt	Gluten free Dairy free	**4**

Chicken Dhansak

6 chicken quarters, skinned

3 onions, quartered

6 garlic cloves, halved

2.5cm (1in) piece fresh root ginger, peeled and roughly chopped

2–3 red chillies, seeded, if you like, and chopped (see page 15)

1 tbsp coriander seeds

1 tbsp cumin seeds

5 black peppercorns

seeds from 4 cardamom pods

2 tsp ground turmeric

2 tsp ground cinnamon

3 tbsp ghee or oil

175g (6oz) masoor dal (red split lentils)

175g (6oz) chana dal

3 tomatoes, peeled and finely chopped (see page 18)

1 tsp salt

3 small thin aubergines, or 1 medium one

1 tbsp dark brown sugar

2 tbsp lemon juice

salt and ground black pepper

1 Cut each chicken quarter into two or three pieces. Put the onions, garlic, ginger and chillies in a food processor or blender with 2 tbsp water. Process until very finely chopped. Add the spices and process again.

2 Heat the ghee or oil in a large flameproof, heavy-based casserole. Add the spice paste and cook over a medium heat, stirring frequently, for about 10 minutes or until the onion is softened and golden brown. Add the chicken, increase the heat and cook, turning, for a few minutes to seal.

3 Add the dals to the casserole with the tomatoes and cook for 2 minutes, stirring all the time. Add enough water to just cover the dal and the chicken and bring to the boil. Lower the heat, add the salt, then cover and simmer for 20 minutes.

4 Halve the small aubergines (or cut the medium one into large chunks). Add to the dhansak with the sugar and lemon juice. Re-cover and simmer for a further 20–30 minutes or until the chicken is tender and the lentils are mushy. Check from time to time to make sure that the dhansak is not sticking to the base of the pan – add a little extra water if it starts to look too dry.

5 Using a potato masher, mash the dals to break them down slightly. Check the seasoning and serve.

EASY		NUTRITIONAL INFORMATION		Serves
Preparation Time 20 minutes	**Cooking Time** 1 hour	**Per Serving** 554 calories, 19g fat (of which 8g saturates), 42g carbohydrate, 1.1 salt	Gluten free Dairy free	**6**

Beef, Pork and Lamb

Beef Jambalaya

Smoky Pimento Goulash

Mexican Chilli Con Carne

Thai Beef Curry

Spicy Beef Madras

Jamaican-spiced Pork Steaks

Pork Vindaloo

Curried Lamb with Lentils

Lamb Biryani

Lamb Korma with Red Onion Cachumber

Lamb and Bamboo Shoot Red Curry

Lamb, Potato and Peanut Curry

Lamb Pasanda

Lamb Rogan Josh

Beef Jambalaya

275g (10oz) fillet steak, cut into thin strips

4 tsp mild chilli powder

1 tsp ground black pepper

about 5 tbsp oil

150g (5oz) chorizo sausage, sliced and cut into strips, or 125g (4oz) cubed sausage

2 celery sticks, cut into 5cm (2in) strips

2 red peppers, cut into 5cm (2in) strips

150g (5oz) onions, roughly chopped

2 garlic cloves, crushed

275g (10oz) long-grain white rice

1 tbsp tomato purée

1 tbsp ground ginger

2 tsp Cajun seasoning

900ml (1½ pints) beef stock

8 large cooked prawns, peeled and deveined (see page 22)

salt

mixed salad to serve

1 Put the steak into a plastic bag with 1 tsp chilli powder and the black pepper. Seal and shake to mix.

2 Heat 1 tbsp oil in a large heavy-based frying pan and cook the chorizo or sausage until golden. Add the celery and peppers to the pan and cook for 3–4 minutes until just beginning to soften and brown. Remove from the pan and put to one side. Add 2 tbsp of the oil to the pan and fry the steak in batches; put to one side and keep warm.

3 Add a little more oil to the pan, if needed, and cook the onions until transparent. Add the garlic, rice, tomato purée, remaining chilli powder, ground ginger and Cajun seasoning, then cook for 2 minutes until the rice turns translucent.

4 Stir in the stock, season with salt and bring to the boil. Cover and simmer for about 20 minutes, stirring occasionally, until the rice is tender and most of the liquid has been absorbed (add a little more water during cooking if needed).

5 Add the reserved steak, chorizo, red peppers and celery, and the prawns. Heat gently, stirring, until piping hot. Adjust the seasoning and serve with a mixed salad.

EASY		NUTRITIONAL INFORMATION		Serves
Preparation Time 10 minutes	**Cooking Time** 40 minutes	**Per Serving** 554 calories, 30g fat (of which 9g saturates), 40g carbohydrate, 1.8g salt	Dairy free	**4**

Get Ahead

To prepare ahead Complete the recipe. Cool and chill (it will keep for up to three days) or freeze (it will keep for up to one month).

To use If frozen, thaw overnight at a cool room temperature. Return the goulash to the casserole, bring to the boil and simmer gently for 15–20 minutes until piping hot, adding 100ml (3½fl oz) hot beef stock if it looks dry.

Smoky Pimento Goulash

3 tbsp olive oil

1.1kg (2½lb) braising steak, cut into large cubes

16 shallots or button onions

225g (8oz) piece chorizo sausage, roughly chopped

1 red chilli, seeded and finely chopped (see page 15)

3 bay leaves

3 garlic cloves, crushed

2 tbsp plain flour

2 tbsp smoked paprika

700g jar tomato passata

100ml (3½fl oz) hot beef stock

salt and ground black pepper

For the minted soured cream

284ml carton soured cream

1 tbsp finely chopped fresh mint

1 tbsp extra virgin olive oil, plus extra to drizzle

1 Mix together all the ingredients for the minted soured cream and season with a little salt and plenty of pepper. Cover and chill until needed. Preheat the oven to 170°C (150°C fan oven) mark 3.

2 Heat the olive oil in a 4 litre (7 pint) flameproof casserole until very hot. Brown the beef, a few cubes at a time, over a high heat until it is deep brown all over. Remove with a slotted spoon and set aside. Repeat with the remaining beef.

3 Reduce the heat under the casserole, then add the onions, chorizo, chilli, bay leaves and garlic. Fry for 7–10 minutes until the onions are golden brown and beginning to soften. Return the meat to the casserole and stir in the flour and paprika. Cook, stirring, for 1–2 minutes, then add the passata. Season, cover and cook in the oven for 2½ hours or until the beef is meltingly tender. Check halfway through cooking – if the beef looks dry, add the hot beef stock. Serve with the minted soured cream, drizzled with a little olive oil and a grinding of black pepper.

Serves	EASY			NUTRITIONAL INFORMATION	
8	**Preparation Time** 20 minutes	**Cooking Time** about 3 hours		**Per Serving** 515 calories, 35g fat (of which 14g saturates), 13g carbohydrate, 1.3g salt	Dairy free

Cook's Tips

Instead of a can of tomatoes with garlic, use a can of chopped tomatoes and 1 crushed garlic clove.

Adding a little dark chocolate to chilli con carne brings out the flavours of this tasty dish.

2 tbsp olive oil

450g (1lb) minced beef

1 large onion, finely chopped

1 tsp each hot chilli powder and ground cumin

3 tbsp tomato purée

300ml (½ pint) hot vegetable stock

400g can chopped tomatoes with garlic (see Cook's Tips)

25g (1oz) dark chocolate

400g can red kidney beans, drained and rinsed

2 x 20g packs fresh coriander, chopped

salt and ground black pepper

guacamole, salsa, soured cream, grated cheese, tortilla chips and pickled chillies to serve

Mexican Chilli Con Carne

1 Heat 1 tbsp oil in a large non-stick pan and fry the beef for 10 minutes until well browned, stirring to break up any lumps. Remove from the pan with a slotted spoon and set aside.

2 Add the remaining oil to the pan, then fry the onion, stirring, for 10 minutes until soft and golden.

3 Add the spices and fry for 1 minute, then return the beef to the pan. Add the tomato purée, stock and tomatoes. Bring to the boil, then reduce to a simmer. Continue to bubble gently, uncovered, for 35–40 minutes, or until the sauce is well reduced and the mixture is quite thick.

4 Stir in the chocolate, kidney beans and coriander, season with salt and pepper, then simmer for 5 minutes.

5 Serve with guacamole, salsa, soured cream, grated cheese, tortilla chips and pickled chillies.

EASY		NUTRITIONAL INFORMATION		Serves
Preparation Time 5 minutes	**Cooking Time** about 1 hour	**Per Serving** 408 calories, 19.2g fat (of which 6.7g saturates), 28.2g carbohydrate, 1.1g salt	Gluten free Dairy free	**4**

Thai Beef Curry

4 cloves

1 tsp coriander seeds

1 tsp cumin seeds

seeds from 3 cardamom pods

2 garlic cloves, roughly chopped

2.5cm (1in) piece fresh root ginger, peeled and roughly chopped

1 small onion, roughly chopped

2 tbsp sunflower oil

1 tbsp sesame oil

1 tbsp Thai red curry paste

1 tsp turmeric

450g (1lb) sirloin steak, cut into 3cm (1¼in) cubes

225g (8oz) potatoes, quartered

4 tomatoes, quartered

1 tsp sugar

1 tbsp light soy sauce

300ml (½ pint) coconut milk

150ml (¼ pint) beef stock

4 small red chillies, bruised (see page 15)

50g (2oz) cashew nuts

roasted chillies to garnish (optional)

rice and stir-fried green vegetables to serve

1 Put the cloves, coriander, cumin and cardamom seeds into a small heavy-based frying pan and fry over a high heat for 1–2 minutes until the spices release their aroma. Be careful that they do not burn. Leave to cool slightly, then grind to a powder in a spice grinder or blender.

2 Put the garlic, ginger and onion into a blender or food processor and whiz to form a smooth paste. Heat the sunflower and sesame oils in a wok or deep frying pan. Add the onion purée and the curry paste and stir-fry for 5 minutes, then add the ground roasted spices and the turmeric and fry for a further 5 minutes.

3 Add the beef to the pan and fry for 5 minutes or until browned on all sides. Add the potatoes, tomatoes, sugar, soy sauce, coconut milk, stock and chillies. Bring to the boil, then reduce the heat, cover the pan and simmer gently for about 15 minutes or until the beef is tender and the potatoes are cooked.

4 Stir in the cashew nuts and serve the curry with rice and stir-fried vegetables, garnished with a roasted red chilli, if you like.

Serves 4	A LITTLE EFFORT		NUTRITIONAL INFORMATION	
	Preparation Time 20 minutes, plus cooling	**Cooking Time** about 30 minutes	**Per Serving** 443 calories, 26g fat (of which 7g saturates), 23g carbohydrate, 1.2g salt	Gluten free Dairy free

1¹/₂ tsp chilli powder

2 tsp ground coriander

2 tsp ground turmeric

¹/₄ tsp ground ginger

¹/₄ tsp ground pepper

300ml (¹/₂ pint) thin coconut milk

4 tbsp ghee or vegetable oil

2 onions, chopped

2 garlic cloves, crushed

900g (2lb) well-trimmed stewing beef,
cut into 2.5cm (1in) cubes

300ml (¹/₂ pint) beef stock

lemon juice

salt

Spicy Beef Madras

1 Mix the spices and pepper to a paste with a little of
the coconut milk. Set aside. Heat the ghee or oil in a
large, heavy-based pan or flameproof casserole, add
the onions and garlic and fry gently for 5 minutes or
until soft and lightly coloured. Add the spicy paste
and fry, stirring constantly, for another 3–4 minutes.

2 Add the meat and stock to the pan and bring slowly
to the boil. Cover and simmer gently for about
1¹/₂ hours or until tender.

3 Add the remaining coconut milk with lemon juice
and salt to taste. Bring to the boil, lower the heat
and simmer for 8–10 minutes until slightly thickened.
Serve at once.

Serves 6	EASY		NUTRITIONAL INFORMATION	
	Preparation Time 10 minutes	**Cooking Time** 1¾ hours	**Per Serving** 381 calories, 24g fat (of which 17g saturates), 6g carbohydrate, 0.9g salt	Gluten free Dairy free

Try Something Different

Instead of the **spring-onion butter**, brush 16 spring onions lightly with oil and barbecue or grill for 5 minutes. Squeeze some fresh lime juice on top (saves 30 calories per serving) and serve with the corn.

Jamaican-spiced Pork Steaks

2 garlic cloves, crushed

2 small red chillies, finely chopped (including seeds) (see page 15)

1 tsp ground allspice

2 tbsp dark rum

2 tbsp tomato ketchup

4 pork steaks, each weighing about 200g (7oz)

50g (2oz) butter, softened

2 spring onions, thinly sliced

4 corn cobs

salt and ground black pepper

1 Mix together the garlic, chillies, allspice, rum and tomato ketchup. Brush all over the pork steaks, cover and chill for at least 30 minutes or overnight.

2 Mix the butter with the spring onions and plenty of black pepper; put to one side.

3 Preheat the barbecue or grill. Cook the corn cobs in lightly salted boiling water for 2 minutes. Drain well, then barbecue or grill until cooked and beginning to char – about 4–5 minutes. Barbecue or grill the pork for about 5 minutes on each side until cooked through. Serve with the corn, smothered in the spring-onion butter.

EASY		NUTRITIONAL INFORMATION		Serves
Preparation Time 20 minutes, plus marinating	**Cooking Time** 10 minutes	**Per Serving** 562 calories, 20.9g fat (of which 10g saturates), 43.8g carbohydrate, 1.7g salt	Gluten free	**4**

Pork Vindaloo

4 tbsp ghee or vegetable oil

1 large onion, finely sliced

6–8 whole dried red chillies

2 tsp cumin seeds

2 tsp coriander seeds

2 tsp paprika

10 black peppercorns

2.5cm (1in) cinnamon stick

seeds of 6 green cardamom pods

2 tsp mustard seeds

3 whole cloves

2.5cm (1in) piece fresh root ginger, peeled and chopped

10 garlic cloves

1 tsp salt

6 tbsp wine vinegar

2 tbsp tomato purée

900g (2lb) well-trimmed pork shoulder, cut into 2.5cm (1in) cubes

1 Heat half the ghee or oil in a large heavy-based frying pan or flameproof casserole, add the onion and fry over medium heat until just turning brown. Remove the onion from the casserole with a slotted spoon and put in a blender or food processor. Add the chillies to the machine with the spices, garlic, salt, vinegar, tomato purée and 4 tbsp water. Whiz until smooth.

2 Heat the remaining ghee or oil in the pan, add the pork and fry over medium heat until browned on all sides. Add the onion and spice mixture and cook for a few minutes over high heat, stirring all the time to prevent sticking.

3 Reduce the heat to very low, cover and cook very gently for about 1½ hours or until the meat is tender and the sauce considerably reduced. Serve hot.

EASY		NUTRITIONAL INFORMATION		Serves
Preparation Time 15 minutes	**Cooking Time** about 2 hours	**Per Serving** 434 calories, 25g fat (of which 13g saturates), 6g carbohydrate, 1.7g salt	Gluten free	**4**

Curried Lamb with Lentils

500g (1lb 2oz) lean stewing lamb on the bone, cut into
8 pieces (ask your butcher to do this), trimmed of fat

1 tsp ground cumin

1 tsp ground turmeric

2 garlic cloves, crushed

1 medium red chilli, seeded and chopped (see page 15)

2.5cm (1in) piece fresh root ginger, peeled and grated

2 tbsp vegetable oil

1 onion, chopped

400g can chopped tomatoes

2 tbsp vinegar

175g (6oz) red lentils, rinsed

salt and ground black pepper

coriander sprigs to garnish

rocket salad to serve

1 Put the lamb into a shallow, sealable container, add the spices, garlic, chilli, ginger, salt and pepper. Stir well to mix, then cover and chill for at least 30 minutes.

2 Heat the oil in a large flameproof casserole, add the onion and cook over a low heat for 5 minutes. Add the lamb and cook for 10 minutes, turning regularly, until the meat is evenly browned.

3 Add the tomatoes, vinegar, 450ml (¾ pint) boiling water and the lentils and bring to the boil. Reduce the heat, cover and simmer for 1 hour. Remove the lid and cook for 30 minutes, stirring occasionally, until the sauce is thick and the lamb is tender. Serve hot, garnished with coriander, with a rocket salad.

Serves 4	EASY		NUTRITIONAL INFORMATION	
	Preparation Time 15 minutes, plus marinating	**Cooking Time** 1 hour 50 minutes	**Per Serving** 478 calories, 21.5g fat (of which 7.4g saturates), 36.3g carbohydrate, 0.3g salt	Gluten free Dairy free

1 onion, roughly chopped

2 garlic cloves

2.5cm (1in) piece fresh root ginger, peeled and roughly chopped

150ml (¼ pint) ghee or vegetable oil

450g (1lb) boned shoulder of lamb, cubed

150ml (¼ pint) natural yogurt

50g (2oz) ground almonds

4 whole cloves

6 green cardamom pods

1 tsp cumin seeds

2.5cm (1in) cinnamon stick

450g (1lb) basmati rice, rinsed (see page 25) and well drained

50g (2oz) sultanas

1–2 tsp salt

large pinch of saffron threads, soaked in 4 tbsp boiling water

crisp browned onions, to garnish

Lamb Biryani

1 Put the onion, garlic and ginger in a blender and whiz until smooth. Heat 4 tbsp ghee or oil in a flameproof casserole. Add the lamb and fry over high heat until well browned. Transfer to a plate. Add the onion purée to the the casserole and fry, stirring, over high heat for 2 minutes. Return the meat to the casserole, then stir in the yogurt a spoonful at a time. Cook each addition over high heat, stirring, until the yogurt is absorbed. Add the almonds and 150ml (¼ pint) water. Bring to the boil, cover and simmer, stirring occasionally, for 30 minutes. Preheat the oven to 150°C (130°C fan oven) mark 2.

2 Heat the remaining ghee in a heavy-based frying pan, add the dried spices and fry gently for 1 minute. Add the rice, stirring. Stir in the sultanas and salt to taste.

3 Sprinkle the rice evenly over the meat. Add water to just cover. DO NOT STIR. Bring to the boil, cover and cook in the oven for 30 minutes. Drizzle the saffron water over. Recover and bake for 15 minutes. Fork up the meat and rice, and sprinkle with the garnish.

EASY		NUTRITIONAL INFORMATION		Serves
Preparation Time 30 minutes	**Cooking Time** 1¾ hours	**Per Serving** 722 calories, 39 fat (of which 20g saturates), 70g carbohydrate, 1g salt	Gluten free	**6**

Cook's Tip

Cachumber is a mix of finely chopped fresh vegetables served as an accompaniment to spicy Indian food.

Lamb Korma with Red Onion Cachumber

150g carton natural yogurt

700g (1½lb) boneless lamb, cut into 2.5cm (1in) pieces

1 tbsp golden caster sugar

3 tbsp groundnut oil

1 tsp ground turmeric

2 tsp ground coriander

1 small onion, finely chopped

4 garlic cloves, crushed

1cm (½in) piece fresh root ginger, peeled and finely chopped

1 red onion, finely sliced

1 tomato, seeded and diced

1 tbsp chopped mint, plus extra to garnish (optional)

juice of ½ lime

50g (2oz) ground almonds

150ml (¼ pint) double cream

large pinch of saffron threads

salt and ground black pepper

naan bread to serve

For the korma paste

3 tbsp ground cinnamon

seeds from 36 green cardamom pods

30 cloves

18 bay leaves

1 tbsp fennel seeds

1 tsp salt

1 Put all the ingredients for the korma paste into a food processor and blend to a powder. Tip the powder into a bowl and add 4 tbsp water, stirring well to make a paste. Divide into three equal portions, then freeze two (see Freezing Tip, page 74) and put the other into a large bowl. To make the curry, add the yogurt, lamb and sugar to the paste in the bowl and mix well. Cover the bowl, chill and leave the lamb to marinate for at least 4 hours, preferably overnight.

2 Preheat the oven to 190°C (170°C fan oven) mark 5. Heat the oil in a flameproof casserole, add the turmeric and coriander and fry for 30 seconds. Add the chopped onion and stir-fry over a high heat for 10 minutes until soft. Add the garlic and ginger and cook for 1–2 minutes. Add the lamb, cover the casserole and cook in the oven for 20 minutes.

3 For the red onion cachumber, put the sliced red onion, tomato, mint and lime juice in a bowl and toss. Season well with salt, and chill until needed.

4 Take the casserole out of the oven, and reduce the oven temperature to 170°C (150°C fan oven) mark 3. Add the ground almonds, cream, saffron and 100ml (3½fl oz) water. Season well with salt and pepper and stir together. Cover the casserole, return to the oven and cook for 1½ hours or until the lamb is tender. Serve the lamb korma with naan bread and red onion cachumber, garnished with mint, if you like.

Serves 4	A LITTLE EFFORT		NUTRITIONAL INFORMATION	
	Preparation Time 20 minutes, plus marinating	**Cooking Time** 2 hours	**Per Serving** 714 calories, 56.9g fat (of which 22.2g saturates), 14.9g carbohydrate, 0.5g salt	Gluten free

2 tbsp sunflower oil

1 large onion, cut into wedges

2 garlic cloves, finely chopped

450g (1lb) lean boneless lamb, cut into 3cm (1¼in) cubes

2 tbsp Thai red curry paste

150ml (¼ pint) lamb or beef stock

2 tbsp Thai fish sauce (nam pla)

2 tsp soft brown sugar

200g can bamboo shoots, drained and thinly sliced

1 red pepper, seeded and thinly sliced

2 tbsp freshly chopped mint

1 tbsp freshly chopped basil

25g (1oz) unsalted peanuts, toasted

rice to serve

Lamb and Bamboo Shoot Red Curry

1 Heat the oil in a wok or large frying pan, add the onion and garlic and fry over a medium heat for 5 minutes.

2 Add the lamb and curry paste and stir-fry for 5 minutes. Add the stock, fish sauce and sugar. Bring to the boil, then lower the heat, cover and simmer gently for 20 minutes.

3 Stir the bamboo shoots, red pepper and herbs into the curry and cook, uncovered, for a further 10 minutes. Stir in the peanuts and serve immediately, with rice.

Serves 4	EASY		NUTRITIONAL INFORMATION	
	Preparation Time 10 minutes	**Cooking Time** 45 minutes	**Per Serving** 397 calories, 25g fat (of which 8g saturates), 17g carbohydrate, 0.4g salt	Gluten free Dairy free

Cook's Tip

Massaman paste is a Thai curry paste. The ingredients include red chillies, roasted shallots, roasted garlic, galangal, lemongrass, roasted coriander seeds, roasted cumin, roasted cloves, white pepper, salt and shrimp paste. You will find it in supermarkets or Asian food shops.

Lamb, Potato and Peanut Curry

2 tbsp olive oil

1 medium onion, chopped

1 tbsp peeled and grated fresh root ginger

1.6kg (3½lb) leg of lamb, diced

3–4 tbsp Massaman paste (see Cook's Tip)

1 tbsp Thai fish sauce (nam pla)

2 tbsp peanut butter

100g (3½oz) ground almonds

400ml can coconut milk

600ml (1 pint) hot chicken stock

1–2 tbsp dry sherry

500g (1lb 2oz) small potatoes, peeled and quartered

200g (7oz) green beans, trimmed

75g (3oz) toasted peanuts, roughly chopped

20g pack fresh coriander, finely chopped

2 limes, quartered

rice to serve

1 Preheat the oven to 170°C (150°C fan oven) mark 3. Heat the oil in a large flameproof casserole. Add the onion and cook over a medium heat for 7–8 minutes until golden. Add the ginger and cook for 1 minute. Spoon the onion mixture out of the pan and set aside. Add the lamb and fry in batches until browned. Put to one side.

2 Add the Massaman paste, fish sauce and peanut butter to the casserole and fry for 2–3 minutes, then add the reserved onion and ginger mixture, lamb pieces, the ground almonds, coconut milk, hot stock and sherry.

3 Bring to the boil, then cover with a lid and cook in the oven for 1 hour. Add the potatoes and cook for a further 40 minutes, uncovered, adding the green beans for the last 20 minutes. Garnish the curry with toasted peanuts and coriander. Serve with freshly cooked rice and lime wedges to squeeze over the curry.

EASY		NUTRITIONAL INFORMATION		Serves
Preparation Time 20 minutes	**Cooking Time** about 2 hours	**Per Serving** 664 calories, 47g fat (of which 20g saturates), 19g carbohydrate, 0.5g salt	Gluten free Dairy free	**8**

Cook's Tips

To toast nuts and seeds, put the nuts or seeds in a heavy-based frying pan and dry-fry over a gentle heat until just golden brown. Remove from the pan and cool. Toast nuts and seeds separately.

It is important to ensure that the meat, nuts and onions are thoroughly browned, or the sauce will look insipid rather than rich in colour.

Lamb Pasanda

50g (2oz) blanched almonds, toasted (see Cook's Tips)

50g (2oz) unsalted cashew nuts, toasted

2 tbsp sesame seeds, toasted

2.5cm (1in) piece fresh root ginger, peeled and roughly chopped

2 garlic cloves

2 tbsp ghee or vegetable oil

2 onions, thinly sliced

2 tsp ground cumin

2 tsp ground coriander

½ tsp ground turmeric

½ tsp ground cardamom

½ tsp ground cloves

700g (1½lb) lean boneless lamb, cubed

150ml (¼ pint) double cream

150ml (¼ pint) coconut milk

2 tbsp lemon juice

salt

1 Tip the toasted nuts into a blender or food processor and whiz briefly until finely chopped. Add the sesame seeds, ginger, garlic and 1 tbsp water and whiz to make a purée.

2 Heat the ghee or oil in a large pan, add the onions and cook over a fairly high heat until tinged with brown. Add the nut mixture and cook over a medium-high heat for 2 minutes.

3 Add the ground spices to the pan and cook, stirring, for 2 minutes. Add the meat and cook over a high heat, turning constantly, until browned and sealed on all sides.

4 Add the cream, coconut milk and 150ml (¼ pint) water. Stir in the lemon juice and season with salt to taste. Bring slowly to the boil, then lower the heat and simmer very gently for about 1½ hours or until the lamb is tender.

Serves 4	EASY		NUTRITIONAL INFORMATION	
	Preparation Time 20 minutes	**Cooking Time** 2 hours	**Per Serving** 732 calories, 58g fat (of which 21g saturates), 11g carbohydrate, 0.7g salt	Gluten free

1 red and 1 green pepper, halved and seeded

75ml (2½fl oz) ghee or oil

2 onions, thinly sliced

1 large garlic clove, crushed

2.5cm (1in) piece fresh root ginger,
peeled and finely chopped

4 green cardamom pods, crushed

2 tsp ground turmeric

2 tsp ground coriander

2 tsp paprika

½ tsp chilli powder

900g (2lb) lamb fillet, trimmed and cut into cubes

300ml (½ pint) natural yogurt

6 ripe tomatoes, peeled and chopped (see page 18)

salt

Lamb Rogan Josh

1 Chop half the red and green peppers. Slice the remainder into thin strips. Heat 50ml (2fl oz) ghee or oil in a heavy-based pan or flameproof casserole, add the onions, garlic and ginger and fry gently for 5 minutes or until soft. Add the spices and fry for 2 minutes, stirring constantly. Increase the heat to medium, add the meat and brown on all sides.

2 Reserve 4 tbsp of the yogurt. Add the remainder to the pan, a spoonful at a time. Cook each addition over high heat, stirring, until the yogurt is absorbed. Add salt, the chopped peppers and two-thirds of the tomatoes, increase the heat and fry, stirring, until the juices run. Put a double thickness of foil over the top of the pan and seal with the lid. Simmer, stirring occasionally, for 1½ hours or until the meat is tender.

3 Heat the remaining ghee in a frying pan, add the pepper strips and fry over gentle heat until softened. Add the remaining tomatoes with a pinch of salt, increase the heat and stir. Serve the curry with the pepper mixture on top, drizzled with the yogurt.

EASY		NUTRITIONAL INFORMATION		Serves
Preparation Time 30 minutes	**Cooking Time** 2 hours	**Per Serving** 618 calories, 37g fat (of which 13g saturates), 21g carbohydrate, 0.8g salt	Gluten free	**4**

Fish

Chilli Prawns with Sweet Chilli Sauce

Thai Fishcakes with Chilli Mayo

Lime and Chilli Swordfish

Scallops with Ginger

Coconut Fish Pilau

Seafood Gumbo

Fish Masala

Prawn Madras with Coconut Chutney

Kerala Fish Curry

Salmon and Coconut Curry

Salmon Laksa Curry

Thai Green Shellfish Curry

Thai Red Seafood Curry

Chilli Prawns with Sweet Chilli Sauce

6 tbsp groundnut oil

200ml (7fl oz) coconut milk

2 tsp mild chilli powder

3 garlic cloves, finely chopped

30 raw prawns, peeled and deveined (see page 22), with tail left on

salt and ground black pepper

For the sweet chilli sauce

1 tbsp olive oil

2 large garlic cloves, finely chopped

2 tsp tomato purée

550g (1¼lb) tomatoes, cut into chunks

4 large red chillies, seeded and finely chopped

200g (7oz) dark muscovado sugar

100ml (3½fl oz) white wine vinegar

1 In a large bowl, mix together the groundnut oil, coconut milk, chilli powder, garlic and ½ tsp each of salt and pepper. Add the prawns, tossing to coat evenly. Cover and marinate for at least 2 hours at room temperature or overnight in the fridge.

2 Meanwhile, make the chilli sauce. Heat the olive oil in a pan, add the garlic and tomato purée and cook for 30 seconds. Add the tomatoes, chillies, sugar and vinegar. Bring to the boil and bubble for 30–35 minutes until reduced and pulpy. Pour the tomato mixture into a sieve and, using the back of a ladle, push through as much of the pulp as possible. Return to the pan and simmer for 5 minutes. Add salt to taste. Set aside.

3 Preheat the barbecue or grill. Soak six wooden skewers in water for 20 minutes. Thread five prawns on each skewer and barbecue or grill for 3–4 minutes on each side, basting with the marinade. Serve with the chilli sauce, for dipping.

Serves 6	EASY		NUTRITIONAL INFORMATION	
	Preparation Time 30 minutes, plus soaking and marinating	**Cooking Time** 50 minutes	**Per Serving** 211 calories, 4g fat (of which 1g saturates), 38g carbohydrate, 0.2g salt	Gluten free Dairy free

1 bunch of spring onions

2.5cm (1in) piece fresh root ginger, peeled and roughly chopped

1 lemongrass stalk, roughly chopped

20g pack fresh coriander

½ red chilli, seeded (see page 15)

1 tsp Thai fish sauce (nam pla) (optional)

150ml (¼ pint) mayonnaise

75g (3oz) fresh white breadcrumbs

225g (8oz) skinless haddock

225g (8oz) cooked and peeled prawns

oil for frying

2 tbsp Thai sweet chilli sauce

20g pack basil, roughly chopped

1 fat garlic clove, crushed (optional)

strips of red chilli to garnish

2 limes, cut into wedges, and 120g bag baby leaf spinach to serve

Thai Fishcakes with Chilli Mayo

1 Put the spring onions, ginger, lemongrass, coriander, chilli and fish sauce, if using, in a food processor and blend to a rough paste. Add 3 tbsp mayonnaise, the breadcrumbs, haddock and prawns and blend for 5 seconds.

2 With wet hands, shape the mixture into eight patties, each about 5cm (2in) in diameter.

3 Heat a drizzle of oil in a non-stick frying pan. Fry the patties in two batches for 3–4 minutes on each side until crisp and golden.

4 Mix the sweet chilli sauce, basil and garlic, if using, into the remaining mayonnaise. Serve with the fishcakes, red chilli strips, lime wedges and spinach leaves.

EASY		NUTRITIONAL INFORMATION		Serves
Preparation Time 25 minutes	**Cooking Time** 8–10 minutes	**Per Serving** 554 calories, 44g fat (of which 5.9g saturates), 17.3g carbohydrate, 1.3g salt	Dairy free	**4**

1 tsp dried chilli flakes

4 tbsp olive oil

grated zest and juice of 1 lime, plus 1 whole lime, sliced, to serve

1 garlic clove, crushed

4 x 175g (6oz) swordfish steaks

salt and ground black pepper

mixed salad to serve

Lime and Chilli Swordfish

1 Put the chilli flakes in a large shallow bowl. Add the oil, lime zest and juice and garlic, and mix everything together. Add the swordfish steaks to the marinade and toss several times to coat completely. Leave to marinate for 30 minutes.

2 Preheat the barbecue or preheat a griddle until hot.

3 Lift the swordfish out of the marinade, season well with salt and pepper, and then cook the steaks for 2 minutes on each side. Top with slices of lime and continue to cook for 1 minute or until the fish is opaque right through. Serve immediately, with a mixed salad.

Serves	EASY			NUTRITIONAL INFORMATION	
4	**Preparation Time** 10 minutes, plus marinating	**Cooking Time** 5 minutes		**Per Serving** 216 calories, 10g fat (of which 2g saturates), 0g carbohydrate, 0.6g salt	Gluten free Dairy free

Scallops with Ginger

2 tbsp vegetable oil

500g (1lb 2oz) shelled large scallops, cut into 5mm (¼in) slices

4 celery sticks, sliced diagonally

1 bunch of spring onions, sliced diagonally

25g (1oz) piece fresh root ginger, peeled and shredded

2 large garlic cloves, sliced

¼ tsp chilli powder

2 tbsp lemon juice

2 tbsp light soy sauce

3 tbsp freshly chopped coriander

salt and ground black pepper

rice to serve

1 Heat the oil in a wok or large frying pan. Add the scallops, celery, spring onions, ginger, garlic and chilli powder and stir-fry over a high heat for 2 minutes or until the vegetables are just tender.

2 Pour in the lemon juice and soy sauce, allow to bubble up, then stir in about 2 tbsp chopped coriander and season with salt and pepper. Sprinkle with the remaining coriander and serve with rice.

EASY		NUTRITIONAL INFORMATION		Serves
Preparation Time 15 minutes	**Cooking Time** 3 minutes	**Per Serving** 197 calories, 7g fat (of which 1g saturates), 6g carbohydrate, 2g salt	Dairy free	**4**

Seafood Gumbo

125g (4oz) butter
50g (2oz) plain flour
1–2 tbsp Cajun spice
1 onion, chopped
1 green pepper, seeded and chopped
5 spring onions, sliced
1 tbsp freshly chopped flat-leafed parsley
1 garlic clove, crushed
1 beef tomato, chopped
125g (4oz) garlic sausage, finely sliced
75g (3oz) American easy-cook rice
1.1 litres (2 pints) vegetable stock
250g (9oz) okra, sliced
1 bay leaf and 1 fresh thyme sprig
juice of ½ lemon
4 cloves
175g (6oz) each raw tiger prawns and mussels in their shells, cleaned (see page 22)
150g (5oz) squid tubes, sliced
salt, cayenne and ground black pepper

1 Heat the butter in a 2.6 litre (4½ pint) heavy-based pan over a low heat. Add the flour and Cajun spice and cook, stirring, for 1–2 minutes until golden brown. Add the onion, green pepper, spring onions, parsley and garlic and cook for 5 minutes.

2 Add the tomato, garlic sausage and rice to the pan and stir well to coat. Add the stock, okra, bay leaf, thyme, 2 tsp salt, ¼ tsp cayenne pepper, lemon juice and cloves. Season with black pepper. Bring to the boil and simmer, covered, for 12 minutes or until the rice is tender.

3 Add the seafood and cook for 3–4 minutes, until the prawns are pink and the mussels have opened. Discard any mussels that are still closed. Serve the gumbo in deep bowls.

Cook's Tip

- -

Gumbo is a traditional stew from the southern states of the USA, containing meat, vegetables and shellfish and thickened with okra.

EASY		NUTRITIONAL INFORMATION		Serves
Preparation Time 20 minutes	**Cooking Time** 30 minutes	**Per Serving** 607 calories, 38.1g fat (of which 21.2g saturates), 41.8g carbohydrate, 1.6g salt	Gluten free	**4**

Try Something Different

There are plenty of alternatives to cod: try coley (saithe), sea bass or pollack.

Coconut Fish Pilau

2 tsp olive oil

1 shallot, chopped

1 tbsp Thai green curry paste

225g (8oz) brown basmati rice, rinsed (see page 25)

600ml (1 pint) hot fish or vegetable stock

150ml (¼ pint) half-fat coconut milk

350g (12oz) skinless cod fillet, cut into bite-size pieces

350g (12oz) sugarsnap peas

125g (4oz) cooked and peeled prawns

25g (1oz) flaked almonds, toasted (see Cook's Tips, page 108)

squeeze of lemon juice

salt and ground black pepper

2 tbsp freshly chopped coriander to garnish

1 Heat the oil in a frying pan, add the shallot and 1 tbsp water and fry for 4–5 minutes until golden. Stir in the curry paste and cook for 1–2 minutes.

2 Add the rice, hot stock and coconut milk. Bring to the boil, then cover and simmer for 15–20 minutes until all the liquid has been absorbed.

3 Add the cod and cook for 3–5 minutes. Add the sugarsnap peas, prawns, almonds and lemon juice and stir over the heat for 3–4 minutes until heated through. Check the seasoning and serve immediately, garnished with coriander.

Serves	EASY		NUTRITIONAL INFORMATION	
4	**Preparation Time** 15 minutes	**Cooking Time** 30 minutes	**Per Serving** 398 calories, 7g fat (of which 1g saturates), 53g carbohydrate, 0.4g salt	Gluten free Dairy free

1 onion, quartered

2 garlic cloves

1–2 hot green chillies, halved, seeds removed, if you like (see page 15)

2.5cm (1in) piece fresh root ginger, peeled and halved

4 tbsp freshly chopped coriander

juice of 2 limes

1 tbsp coriander seeds

1 tsp fenugreek seeds

1 tsp ground turmeric

2 tbsp vegetable oil

5 large juicy tomatoes, peeled and chopped (see page 18)

1 tbsp garam masala (see page 11)

4 white fish steaks, such as cod, haddock, halibut

about 2 tbsp plain white flour, for coating

oil for shallow-frying

salt

Fish Masala

1 Put the onion, garlic, chillies, ginger, chopped coriander and lime juice in a blender or food processor and whiz to make a fairly thick paste. Crush the coriander and fenugreek seeds using a pestle and mortar, then add to the spice paste with the turmeric and mix well.

2 Heat the oil in a large frying pan. Add the spice paste and cook, stirring constantly, for 5 minutes. Stir in the chopped tomatoes, garam masala and salt to taste. Cook for about 5 minutes or until the tomatoes have broken down and their liquid has evaporated.

3 Coat the fish steaks with the flour. Heat the oil in another frying pan. Add the fish steaks and quickly brown on both sides. Transfer the fish steaks to the frying pan containing the sauce, arranging them in a single layer. Spoon a little of the sauce over each fish steak and cover the pan with a lid or a baking sheet. Simmer gently for 8–10 minutes, depending on the thickness of the fish, until the fish is cooked right through. Serve.

EASY		NUTRITIONAL INFORMATION		Serves
Preparation Time 15 minutes	**Cooking Time** about 20 minutes	**Per Serving** 328 calories, 16g fat (of which 2g saturates), 12g carbohydrate, 0.6g salt	Dairy free	**4**

Prawn Madras with Coconut Chutney

2 tbsp groundnut oil

1 medium onion, finely sliced

1 green chilli, seeded and finely chopped (see page 15)

600ml (1 pint) vegetable stock

450g (1lb) raw king prawns, peeled and deveined (see page 22)

2 bay leaves

fresh coriander leaves to garnish

basmati rice to serve

For the Madras paste

1 small onion, finely chopped

2.5cm (1in) piece fresh root ginger, peeled and finely chopped

2 garlic cloves, crushed

juice of $\frac{1}{2}$ lemon

1 tbsp each cumin seeds and coriander seeds

1 tsp cayenne pepper

2 tsp each ground turmeric and garam masala (see page 11)

1 tsp salt

For the coconut chutney

1 tbsp groundnut oil

1 tbsp black mustard seeds

1 medium onion, grated

125g (4oz) desiccated coconut

1 red chilli, seeded and diced

1 Put all the ingredients for the Madras paste into a food processor with 2 tbsp water and blend until smooth. Divide the paste into three equal portions, freeze two (see Freezing Tip, page 74) and put the other into a large bowl.

2 To make the coconut chutney, heat the oil in a pan and add the mustard seeds. Cover the pan with a lid and cook over a medium heat until the seeds pop – you'll hear them jumping against the lid. Add the grated onion, coconut and red chilli, and cook for 3–4 minutes to toast the coconut. Remove from the heat and put to one side.

3 To make the curry, heat the oil in a pan, add the onion and fry for 10 minutes or until soft and golden. Add the Madras paste and green chilli, and cook for 5 minutes. Add the stock and bring to the boil. Reduce the heat to a simmer and add the prawns and bay leaves. Cook for 3–5 minutes until the prawns turn pink. Garnish with coriander and serve with the coconut chutney and basmati rice.

Serves 4	A LITTLE EFFORT		NUTRITIONAL INFORMATION	
	Preparation Time 10 minutes	**Cooking Time** 25 minutes	**Per Serving** 415 calories, 30g fat (of which 18g saturates), 15g carbohydrate, 1.8g salt	Gluten free Dairy free

Cook's Tip

- -

Buy banana leaves from Asian shops.

Get Ahead

- -

Make the sauce up to 4 hours ahead.
To use Gently reheat to simmering point before you add
the fish.

Kerala Fish Curry

4 skinless sole or plaice fillets, about 125g (4oz) each

2 tbsp light olive oil

1 onion, thinly sliced

1 large garlic clove, crushed

1 green chilli, slit lengthways, seeds left in

2.5cm (1in) piece fresh root ginger, peeled and grated

1 tsp ground turmeric

1 tbsp garam masala (see page 11) or 12 curry leaves
200ml (7fl oz) coconut milk

1 tbsp freshly squeezed lime juice, white wine vinegar or
tamarind paste

salt and ground black pepper

fresh banana leaves (optional, see Cook's Tip), basmati
rice and 1 lime, cut into wedges, to serve

1 Roll up the fish fillets from head to tail, and put to
one side.

2 Heat the oil in a deep frying pan over a medium heat
and stir in the onion, garlic, chilli and ginger. Stir for
5–7 minutes until the onion is soft. Add the turmeric
and garam masala or curry leaves and fry for a
further 1–2 minutes until aromatic.

3 Pour the coconut milk into the pan with 200ml (7fl
oz) water and bring to the boil. Reduce the heat and
simmer very gently, uncovered, for 7–10 minutes until
slightly thickened – the consistency of single cream.
Stir in the lime juice, vinegar or tamarind. Check the
seasoning and adjust if necessary.

4 When ready to serve, carefully lower the fish into the
hot sauce and simmer very gently for 1–2 minutes
until just cooked. Serve on a bed of basmati rice, in
deep bowls lined with strips of banana leaves, if you
like, with lime wedges to squeeze over it.

Serves	A LITTLE EFFORT		NUTRITIONAL INFORMATION	
4	**Preparation Time** 10 minutes	**Cooking Time** 20 minutes	**Per Serving** 189 calories, 9g fat (of which 1g saturates), 5g carbohydrate, 0.5g salt	Gluten free Dairy free

Salmon and Coconut Curry

1 tbsp olive oil

1 red onion, sliced

2 tbsp tikka masala curry paste

4 x 100g (3½oz) salmon steaks or pieces of fillet

400ml can coconut milk

juice of 1 lime

handful of coriander, roughly chopped

lime wedges to garnish and boiled rice or naan bread to serve

1 Heat the oil in a pan. Add the onion and cook over a medium heat for 10 minutes or until soft.

2 Add the curry paste to the pan and cook for 1 minute to warm the spices. Add the fish and cook for 2 minutes, turning it once to coat it in the spices.

3 Pour in the coconut milk and bring to the boil, then reduce the heat and simmer for 5 minutes or until the fish is cooked through. Squeeze the lime juice over it and sprinkle with coriander. Serve with lime wedges to squeeze over the fish and boiled rice or naan bread to soak up the creamy sauce.

EASY		NUTRITIONAL INFORMATION		Serves
Preparation Time 2 minutes	**Cooking Time** 18 minutes	**Per Serving** 276 calories, 18.6g fat (of which 3.2g saturates), 8.1g carbohydrate, 0.6g salt	Gluten free Dairy free	**4**

Cook's Tip

Laksa paste is a hot and spicy paste; you could use Thai curry paste instead.

Try Something Different

Instead of the medium rice noodles try using rice vermicelli, or leave out the noodles and serve with basmati rice.

Salmon Laksa Curry

1 tbsp olive oil

1 onion, thinly sliced

3 tbsp laksa paste (see Cook's Tip)

200ml (7fl oz) coconut milk

900ml (1½ pints) hot vegetable stock

200g (7oz) baby sweetcorn, halved lengthways

600g (1lb 5oz) piece skinless salmon fillet, cut into 1cm (½in) slices

225g (8oz) baby leaf spinach

250g (9oz) medium rice noodles

salt and ground black pepper

To garnish

2 spring onions, sliced diagonally

2 tbsp freshly chopped coriander

1 lime, cut into wedges

1 Heat the oil in a wok or large frying pan, then add the onion and fry over a medium heat for 10 minutes, stirring, until golden. Add the laksa paste and cook for 2 minutes.

2 Add the coconut milk, hot stock and sweetcorn, and season with salt and pepper. Bring to the boil, then reduce the heat and simmer for 5 minutes.

3 Add the salmon slices and spinach, stirring to immerse them in the liquid. Cook for 4 minutes or until the fish is opaque all the way through.

4 Meanwhile, put the noodles into a large heatproof bowl, pour boiling water over to cover, and soak for 30 seconds. Drain well, then stir them into the curry. Pour the curry into four warmed bowls and garnish with the spring onions and coriander. Serve immediately with lime wedges.

Serves 4	EASY		NUTRITIONAL INFORMATION	
	Preparation Time 10 minutes	**Cooking Time** 20 minutes	**Per Serving** 570 calories, 22g fat (of which 3g saturates), 55g carbohydrate, 1.9g salt	Gluten free Dairy free

Try Something Different

Use cleaned sliced squid or mussels instead of scallops and prawns.

1 tbsp vegetable oil

1 lemongrass stalk, trimmed and chopped

2 small red chillies, seeded and chopped (see page 15)

a handful of fresh coriander leaves, chopped, plus extra to serve

2 kaffir lime leaves, chopped

1–2 tbsp Thai green curry paste

400ml can coconut milk

450ml (³/₄ pint) vegetable stock

375g (13oz) queen scallops with corals

250g (9oz) raw tiger prawns, peeled and deveined (see page 22), with tails intact

salt and ground black pepper

jasmine rice to serve

Thai Green Shellfish Curry

1 Heat the oil in a wok or large frying pan. Add the lemongrass, chillies, coriander and lime leaves and stir-fry for 30 seconds. Add the curry paste and fry for 1 minute.

2 Add the coconut milk and stock to the wok or pan, and bring to the boil, then reduce the heat and simmer for 5–10 minutes until slightly reduced. Season well with salt and pepper.

3 Add the scallops and tiger prawns and bring to the boil, then reduce the heat and simmer gently for 2–3 minutes until cooked.

4 Divide the rice among six bowls and spoon the curry on top. Sprinkle with chopped coriander and serve immediately.

EASY		NUTRITIONAL INFORMATION		Serves
Preparation Time 10 minutes	**Cooking Time** 10–15 minutes	**Per Serving** 156 calories, 5g fat (of which 1g saturates), 6g carbohydrate, 0.8g salt	Gluten free Dairy free	**6**

Cook's Tip

If you can't find half-fat coconut milk, use half a can of full-fat coconut milk and make up the difference with water or stock. Freeze the remaining milk for up to one month.

1 tbsp vegetable oil

3 tbsp Thai red curry paste

450g (1lb) monkfish tail, boned to make 350g (12oz) fillet, membrane removed, sliced into rounds

350g (12oz) large raw peeled prawns, deveined

400ml can half-fat coconut milk (see Cook's Tip)

200ml (7fl oz) fish stock (nam pla)

juice of 1 lime

1–2 tbsp Thai fish sauce

125g (4oz) mangetouts

3 tbsp fresh coriander, roughly torn

salt and ground black pepper

Thai Red Seafood Curry

1 Heat the oil in a wok or large non-stick frying pan. Add the curry paste and cook for 1–2 minutes.

2 Add the monkfish and prawns and stir well to coat in the curry paste. Add the coconut milk, stock, lime juice and fish sauce. Stir all the ingredients together and bring just to the boil.

3 Add the mangetouts and simmer for 5 minutes or until the mangetouts and fish are tender. Stir in the coriander and check the seasoning, adding salt and pepper to taste. Serve immediately.

Serves 4	EASY		NUTRITIONAL INFORMATION	
	Preparation Time 10 minutes	**Cooking Time** 8–10 minutes	**Per Serving** 252 calories, 8g fat (of which 1g saturates), 9g carbohydrate, 2.2g salt	Gluten free Dairy free

Index

A

aduki beans: chicken, bean and spinach curry 81
allspice 10
aubergines 19
  aubergine and chickpea pilaf 39
  aubergine and pepper balti 60
  dal with aubergine and mushrooms 47

B

balti paste 12, 60
bamboo shoots: lamb and bamboo shoot red curry 106
basmati rice 23, 25
bean thread noodles 24
beans: Caribbean chicken 70
  chicken, bean and spinach curry 81
  Mexican chilli con carne 95
beef: beef jambalaya 93
  Mexican chilli con carne 95
  smoky pimento goulash 94
  spicy beef Madras 98
  Thai beef curry 96
bhajis, onion 42
biryani: lamb biryani 103
  vegetable biryani 64
black-eyed beans: Caribbean chicken 70
boning fish 21
broccoli: potato and broccoli curry 53

C

cardamom 10
Caribbean chicken 70
carrot relish 60
cayenne pepper 10
cellophane noodles 23, 24
cheese: paneer 44
chicken 20–1
  Caribbean chicken 70
  chicken, bean and spinach curry 81
  chicken dhansak 89
  chicken tikka with coconut dressing 69
  chicken tikka masala 79
  easy Thai red chicken curry 84
  fiery mango chicken 73
  hot jungle curry 82
  lime and chilli chicken goujons 37
  mild spiced chicken with quinoa 76
  Moroccan chicken with chickpeas 80
  spiced chicken pilau 77
  tandoori chicken with cucumber raita 74
  Thai green curry 85
chickpeas: aubergine and chickpea pilaf 39
  chickpea curry 56
  Moroccan chicken with chickpeas 80
chillies 10, 15
  chilli chutney 27
  chilli prawns with sweet chilli sauce 112
  lentil chilli 61
  Mexican chilli con carne 95
  oven-baked chilli rice 40
  sweet chilli sauce 35
  Thai fishcakes with chilli

mayo 113
chutney: chilli chutney 27
  coconut chutney 120
  coriander chutney 27, 43
  fresh mango chutney 27
  spiced pepper chutney 27
cinnamon 10
cloves 10
coconut, creamed 13, 51
  coconut rice 26
coconut chutney 120
coconut cream 51
coconut milk 13
  coconut fish pilau 118
  curried coconut and vegetable rice 50
  salmon and coconut curry 123
coconut powder 13
cod: coconut fish pilau 118
  fish masala 119
coriander chutney 27, 43
coriander seeds 10
courgettes: cumin courgettes with paneer 44
crab balls, Thai 35
cucumber raita 74
cumin 10
  cumin courgettes with paneer 44
curried coconut and vegetable rice 50
curried lamb with lentils 102
curry leaves 11
curry powder 11

D

dal with aubergine and mushrooms 47
dry-frying spices 10
duck: crispy duck with hot and sweet dip 87

E

egg noodles 23, 24
eggs: spiced egg pilau 51

F

fenugreek seeds 11
fish 21
  coconut fish pilau 118
  fish masala 119
  Kerala fish curry 122
  lime and chilli swordfish 114
  salmon laksa curry 124
  Thai fishcakes with chilli mayo 113
  Thai red seafood curry 126
five-spice powder 11
flavourings 14–15
fridges, storing food 29
furikake seasoning 11

G

garam masala 11
garlic 15
ginger 14
  scallops with ginger 115
glass noodles 24
goulash, smoky pimento 94
groundnut (peanut) oil 13
gumbo, seafood 117

H

haddock: Thai fishcakes with chilli mayo 113
harissa 12
herbs 16

hot jungle curry 82
hygiene 20, 28

J

Jamaican-spiced pork steaks 99
jambalaya, beef 93
jointing chicken 20–1

K

Kerala fish curry 122
korma, vegetable 63
korma paste 12

L

laksa paste 12
lamb: curried lamb with lentils 102
  lamb and bamboo shoot red curry 106
  lamb biryani 103
  lamb korma with red onion cachumber 104
  lamb pasanda 108
  lamb, potato and peanut curry 107
  lamb rogan josh 109
lemongrass 14
lentils: chicken dhansak 89
  curried lamb with lentils 102
  dal with aubergine and mushrooms 47
  lentil chilli 61
limes: lime and chilli chicken goujons 37
  lime and chilli swordfish 114
long-grain rice 23, 25

M

Madras paste 12
mangoes: fiery mango chicken 73
  fresh mango chutney 27
  melon, mango and cucumber salad 33
massaman paste 13
Mauritian vegetable curry 59
mayonnaise: Thai fishcakes with chilli mayo 113
melon, mango and cucumber salad 33
Mexican chilli con carne 95
monkfish: Thai red seafood curry 126
Moroccan chicken with chickpeas 80
mushrooms, dal with aubergine and 47
mussels 22
  seafood gumbo 117
mustard seeds 11

N

noodles 23, 24
  salmon laksa curry 124
  tofu noodle curry 55
nutmeg 11

O

oil-water spray 61
oils 13
okra: seafood gumbo 117
onions 17
  lamb korma with red onion cachumber 104
  onion bhajis 42

P

pak choi 18

pakoras 43
paneer, cumin courgettes with 44
paprika 11
pastes 12–13
pastry, samosa 41
peppers 19
  aubergine and pepper balti 60
  spiced pepper chutney 27
pilaf, aubergine and chickpea 39
pilau: coconut fish pilau 118
  pilau rice 26
  spiced chicken pilau 77
  spiced egg pilau 51
poppadoms, prawn 36
pork: Jamaican-spiced pork steaks 99
  pork vindaloo 101
potatoes: lamb, potato and peanut curry 107
  potato and broccoli curry 53
  saag aloo 38
poultry 20–1
prawns 22
  chilli prawns with sweet chilli sauce 112
  prawn Madras with coconut chutney 120
  prawn poppadoms 36
  seafood gumbo 117
  Thai fishcakes with chilli mayo 113
  Thai green curry 85
  Thai green shellfish curry 125
  Thai red seafood curry 126

Q

quinoa, mild spiced chicken with 76

R

raita, cucumber 74
red kidney beans: Mexican chilli con carne 95
rice 23, 25–6
  aubergine and chickpea pilaf 39
  beef jambalaya 93
  Caribbean chicken 70
  coconut fish pilau 118
  coconut rice 26
  curried coconut and vegetable rice 50
  lamb biryani 103
  oven-baked chilli rice 40
  pilau rice 26
  saffron rice 26
  spiced chicken pilau 77
  spiced egg pilau 51
  Thai rice 26
  vegetable biryani 64
  warm spiced rice salad 32
rice noodles 23, 24

S

saag aloo 38
saffron 11
  saffron rice 26
salads: melon, mango and cucumber salad 33
  warm spiced rice salad 32
salmon: salmon and coconut curry 123
  salmon laksa curry 124
samosas, vegetable 41
sauces 13
scallops: scallops with ginger

115
  Thai green shellfish curry 125
seafood gumbo 117
sesame oil 13
shallots 17
shellfish 22
  Thai green shellfish curry 125
shopping 28
skinning fish fillets 21
smoky pimento goulash 94
sole: Kerala fish curry 122
soy sauce 13
spice mixes 11
spices 10–11
spinach: chicken, bean and spinach curry 81
  saag aloo 38
spring onions 18
squash 19
star anise 11
storing food 29
swordfish, lime and chilli 114

T

Tabasco sauce 13
tamari 13
tamarind 13
tandoori chicken with cucumber raita 74
tandoori paste 13
teriyaki sauce 13
Thai beef curry 96
Thai crab balls 35
Thai fish sauce 13
Thai fishcakes with chilli mayo 113
Thai fragrant rice 23
Thai green curry 85
Thai green curry paste 13
Thai green shellfish curry 125
Thai red seafood curry 126
Thai rice 26
Thai vegetable curry 58
tikka masala 79
tofu noodle curry 55
tomatoes 18
  chilli chutney 27
  Mexican chilli con carne 95
  smoky pimento goulash 94
turkey curry 86
turmeric 11

V

vegetable oil 13
vegetables 17–19
  curried coconut and vegetable rice 50
  Mauritian vegetable curry 59
  pakoras 43
  Thai vegetable curry 58
  vegetable biryani 64
  vegetable curry 54
  vegetable korma 63
  vegetable samosas 41

W

wasabi paste 13
wheat noodles 23

Y

yogurt: cucumber raita 74

COOKING MEASURES

TEMPERATURE

°C	Fan oven	Gas mark	°C	Fan oven	Gas mark
110	90	¼	190	170	5
130	110	½	200	180	6
140	120	1	220	200	7
150	130	2	230	210	8
170	150	3	240	220	9
180	160	4			

LIQUIDS

Metric	Imperial	Metric	Imperial
5ml	1 tsp	200ml	7fl oz
15ml	1 tbsp	250ml	9fl oz
25ml	1fl oz	300ml	½ pint
50ml	2fl oz	500ml	18fl oz
100ml	3½fl oz	600ml	1 pint
125ml	4fl oz	900ml	1½ pints
150ml	5fl oz / ¼ pint	1 litre	1¾ pints
175ml	6fl oz		

MEASURES

Metric	Imperial	Metric	Imperial
5mm	¼in	10cm	4in
1cm	½in	15cm	6in
2cm	¾in	18cm	7in
2.5cm	1in	20.5cm	8in
3cm	1¼in	23cm	9in
4cm	1½in	25.5cm	10in
5cm	2in	28cm	11in
7.5cm	3in	30.5cm	12in

WEIGHTS

Metric	Imperial	Metric	Imperial
15g	½oz	275g	10oz
25g	1oz	300g	11oz
40g	1½oz	350g	12oz
50g	2oz	375g	13oz
75g	3oz	400g	14oz
100g	3½oz	425g	15oz
125g	4oz	450g	1lb
150g	5oz	550g	1¼lb
175g	6oz	700g	1½lb
200g	7oz	900g	2lb
225g	8oz	1.1kg	2½lb
250g	9oz		

Always remember...

- Ovens and grills must be preheated to the specified temperature.
- For fan ovens the temperature should be set to 20°C less.
- Use one set of measurements; do not mix metric and imperial.
- All spoon measures are level.

NOTES

- Both metric and imperial measures are given for the recipes. Follow either set of measures, not a mixture of both, as they are not interchangeable.
- All spoon measures are level.
  1 tsp = 5ml spoon; 1 tbsp = 15ml spoon.
- Ovens and grills must be preheated to the specified temperature.
- Use sea salt and freshly ground black pepper unless otherwise suggested.
- Fresh herbs should be used unless dried herbs are specified in a recipe.
- Medium eggs should be used except where otherwise specified. Free-range eggs are recommended.
- Note that certain recipes, including mayonnaise, lemon curd and some cold desserts, contain raw or lightly cooked eggs. The young, elderly, pregnant women and anyone with an immune-deficiency disease should avoid these, because of the slight risk of salmonella.
- Calorie, fat and carbohydrate counts per serving are provided for the recipes.
- If you are following a gluten- or dairy-free diet, check the labels on all pre-packaged food goods.
- Recipe serving suggestions do not take gluten- or dairy-free diets into account.

Picture Credits
Photographers: Neil Barclay (pages 37, 78, 80 and 115); Martin Brigdale (pages 55, 83, 85, 97, 106 and 126); Nicki Dowey (pages 32, 33, 34, 36, 38, 40, 50, 51, 52, 58, 60, 75, 77, 87, 94, 95, 99, 102, 105, 107, 112,113, 114, 121, 123, 124 and 125); Will Heap (page 116); William Lingwood (pages 41, 42, 43, 45, 46, 62, 65, 88, 98, 100, 103, 108, 109 and 119); Craig Robertson (all basics photography and pages 39, 59, 61, 68, 72, 81, 84, 92, 118 and 122); Lucinda Symons (pages 54, 57, 76 and 86).
Home Economists: Anna Burges-Lumsden, Joanna Farrow, Emma Jane Frost, Teresa Goldfinch, Alice Hart, Lucy McKelvie, Kim Morphew, Aya Nishimura, Katie Rogers, Bridges Sargeson, Jennifer White and Mari Mererid Williams.
Stylists: Tamzin Ferdinando, Helen Trent and Fanny Ward.